MAGNETISM TO MARRIAGE

Guilt-Free Guide to Dating, Relationships, Premarital Decisions, and Honeymoon

Roy E. Peterson

With the assistance of
Anthony and Kristeena

authorHOUSE®

AuthorHouse™
1663 Liberty Drive
Bloomington, IN 47403
www.authorhouse.com
Phone: 1-800-839-8640

First published by AuthorHouse 4/18/2011

ISBN: 978-1-4567-4345-1 (sc)
ISBN: 978-1-4567-4344-4 (dj)
ISBN: 978-1-4567-4343-7 (e)

Library of Congress Control Number: 2011904229

Printed in the United States of America

Any people depicted in stock imagery provided by Thinkstock are models, and such images are being used for illustrative purposes only. Certain stock imagery © Thinkstock.

This book is printed on acid-free paper.

Dedication

Magnetism to Marriage **is dedicated to Kristeena and Anthony who have taken the next big relationship step and were engaged December 31, 2010. Their long term relationship inspired me to write this book for them, but this is all young couples from the time they start to date to the time they are on their honeymoon.**

Kristeena and Anthony contributed some of the key photos as well as their critique of portions of the manuscript. As the author, I alone take responsibility for the final product and they are to be absolved of any sections or chapters with which they disagreed, but which I felt were important to present using my research, logic, and attempted prose.

Preface

Magnetism to Marriage **is about attraction forces and their role in dating, relationships, and selection of a life mate. Religious relationship chapters are Chapter 1 on Equal Matching, Chapter 8 concerning Premarital Relationships, and Chapter 9 on Christian and Jewish acceptance of Premarital Sex between a committed couple. I use the Romeo and Juliet paradigm for relationships including what to do and what not to do on a date, especially the first.**

What qualifies me to write a Guilt-free Guide to dating and relationships up to marriage? I am <u>not</u> a therapist, psychologist, or psychiatrist. That alone qualifies me. Beyond that I counseled couples as a Deacon in a church, as a military officer talking to young enlisted couples about their plans, and having had both sons and daughters who needed guidance, but were afraid to ask. This practical guide can just be handed to them and if they read it and apply it, they will have a wonderful life.

I find that parents have abdicated their roles in teaching their children about how to relate appropriately, how to love, and how to act with others. Sons and daughters even in the best of marriages do not ask for guidance. Everyone now assumes in the modern era that what kids need, they can get from the Internet or from a Sex Education teacher. The problem is the vast potential for evil and destruction of relationships that the world throws at teenagers and young adults. The things of Satan certainly are pervasive, including misinterpretations of Bible principles. Cast no stones for anyone who engages in premarital sex.

I am not going to lecture anyone on dating and relationship building. That is what I am least qualified to do. I present information, facts, ideas, and concepts so that each person can assess their own situation and work toward a wonderful future in marriage. The true religious perspective makes everything right and obviates the need for the psychologists and psychiatrists.

I find that the best counseling comes from reading both the Old and New Testament Bible. Conflicts, which therapists cannot help one resolve, come from not following Bible precepts. Guilt is that still small voice speaking inside that says you have not obeyed religious teachings. Misplaced guilt comes from religious teachings that have agendas outside what the Bible teaches or does not teach. The farther away we stray the more difficult it is to find the way. Prayer brings back the strength of that little voice and shows us the paths by the still waters. As the Psalmist said, "He restoreth my soul."

Note to Parents: This Guilt-free Guide is objective and open. A pastor, rabbi, or religious leader could not write such a book or else be ready for stoning by his or her congregation. The Catholic Church certainly would not approve of the premarital concepts, nor would fundamental congregations. I take what is in the Bible including teachings about men/women relationships, but have not taken the next step that religious moralists do and twist a scripture or try to pursue a logic or infer a teaching that does not exist.

For the record, I am fundamentalist Southern Baptist. I attended a Baptist University in Texas. I support the proper interpretations of Biblical passages. I do not support profligate sex or deviant sex as it pertains to homosexuality. I do know Jesus forgives such indiscretions and lapses in judgment. I also know that premarital sex is not prohibited in the Bible. Two chapters are specifically devoted to premarital relationships with or without having sexual intercourse. I have no judgment either way and neither should you. Simply put, couples either agree to abstain or have premarital sex. The wedding night is precious either way.

The research and objective views reflected in this book are mine alone and not those of my son, Anthony, or those of his fiancée, Kristeena. In fact Anthony and Kristeena expressed some misgivings with my presentation of facts and biblical interpretations, but that is their right as it is your

right to disagree. I used observations of their long term relationships and my entire purpose for writing this book was to assist them and young couples like them in making choices. You make yours.

Table of Contents

Chapter 1

Matching Equals to Equals

You decide your worth. You deserve the best, but you determine that which is best for you. We all need the best guidance and assistance we can find. The <u>Bible</u> and this <u>Guilt-free Guide</u> are your best friends in finding the one person right for you and molding relationships before marriage and ones that last a lifetime. The goal of dating is living together as man and wife. You do not want to take a chance and jeopardize future happiness for early mistakes.

Those not interested in the religious perspective can go straight to Chapter 2. The truths in here are for everyone to read and apply, not just to Christians or the Jews. I use the religious perspective, because everyone can gain from an appreciation that what is taught is not only religious, but historical and applies to all religious teachings or lack thereof in dealing with relationships and sex.

Be you not unequally yoked... II Corinthians 6:14(NIV)

These words from Paul in writing to the Corinthians, apply to yoking believers to unbelievers, but the principle is important in relationships of any kind, particularly in dating, engagements, and marriages. An unequal yoke of oxen together are a wonderful analogy, because it means the majority of the load is shifted onto the strong one, but the team remains dysfunctional. Unequal yoking destroys both.

1

Equal matching is the key, matching by traits, culture, education, goals, motivations, and a host of physical and mental characteristics.

Everything does not have to match, but the more that do, the higher the probability of success in a relationship and in marriage. Certain traits are recognized in others that we do not each possess. Opposites in thought processes, actions, methods of learning, and other mental ways of considering options do attract because each completes the other. Recognizing these differences and finding the right mate to complement oneself forge a stronger union.

Prayer, Bible reading, Bible study, church attendance, and Christian or Jewish fellowship with wholesome adults (despite their hidden flaws), is foreign to the unbeliever. If one is dating an unbeliever before marriage, then is the time to convert that person. Not after marriage. Happiness comes from sharing God's word and working God's plan. It is true you know -- The family that prays together, stays together. The same is true for a premarital relationship. God is the sun around which lives orbit and stay in balance. The unbeliever is like an unleashed asteroid, spinning through space and hurtling toward some uncertain doom.

> ***....for what fellowship hath righteousness with unrighteousness?***
> ***And what communion hath light with darkness?"***
> ***II Cor.6:14 (KJV)***

Unequal yoking means every job is a chore and unmitigated hardship. Like vision, like goals, like intensity of faith, like mindedness all establish the meaningful relationships and produce a future worth living together. What fellowship indeed can come out of righteousness associating with unrighteousness, but a rotten result? Apples in a barrel touching a rotten apple are soon all rotten. The good apples cannot make the rotten apples better. What communication, or better yet, what kind of communication can there be between light and darkness?

Like sheep we bear the consequences of our decisions to follow the herd whether to pasture or off the cliff. Then we blame God. The prayer then becomes, "Lord, why did you send me this husband or this wife," depending of course on the gender of the person praying. The Lord answers, "I did not provide that husband (or wife). You made the choice. I had another one chosen for you." God will not forsake you in an unequal relationship. Through prayer, I have seen a 50 year old man commit to God, stop drinking, and become a deacon. Not usual, but not impossible. God will make the best of a bad situation through trust in Him and His word. God's mercy deals with our circumstances.

As in all areas of life, God will deal the best He can with the choices that you have made. Marriage is a choice at least in the United States and western nations. Your husband is a choice. Your wife is a choice. When you choose to find your husband or wife with God's help, God will see that you receive the very best. God is good and deals with where we are.

God will provide not only a mate, but the right mate. It is up to us to recognize who that right mate is. I am reminded of an old story about a man, let's call him John, who was a strong Christian living near a large river. John was not rich, but faithful to the Lord. Not having much money, John had faith that God would provide and God always did.

One spring day the river burst its banks and flooded the surrounding fields and town. As the river came up to his doorstep, John waved as the police came by and warned him to evacuate. John told the police, "God will provide." A warning on John's radio said, "Leave the area." John laughed and said aloud, "God will provide." A neighbor leaving his home saw John and said, "I can help you get out of here." John said cheerily, "God will provide, but thanks for the offer."

As the floodwaters rose to mid door level, a rescue boat floated past. "We will help you evacuate," they said over the bullhorn. John shouted back, "The Lord will provide." John had to climb up on the roof of his house. Next a rescue helicopter came by and as it approached, John waved it off with the words that could not be heard from the whirring of the blades, "God will provide."

John drowned. When he got to heaven, John asked Peter to send him immediately to God's throne. John asked, God, "I believed you would provide for me during the flood and now I am dead." God had one of those looks on his face and spoke, "John, I provided for you five times. How many times do I have to provide for you?"

The point of the story is simple. God sends us the right message and right person over and over again crossing our paths, but we have to recognize the right person. God does have someone in mind for you, the right person, the equally matched person, the soul mate. He provided for Adam. He provided for Abraham. He provided for Jacob and Isaac. Ask the Lord, "How will I know?" The likely answer is you already probably know who you need and their characteristics. Do not turn you back on someone who loves you. You do so at your own peril and your life will be unfulfilled.

Going out with an unbeliever, or group of unbelievers is playing with fire. Satan can capture your attention, make you thrill to the flash, raise your libido, and take over your thoughts. I used to laugh when my uncle who was a pastor in a Baptist Church in Texas said, "You can go anywhere where you can still pray. If you think you can pray on a dance floor, then by all means dance. Now, how many of you have prayed while dancing? Raise your hands." Not one person in the congregation did. The point is just going out is not good enough. An individual can influence you to do things you would not otherwise do. A person can capture the imagination and influence feelings. Even good manners can be corrupted by exciting behavior.

Every high school has them. Every college and university has them. "Them" are those boys or girls who want to have sex with every girl or boy they want. I grew up in a small high school town. I remember one of "them" in particular who especially wanted to sleep with "churchgoing" girls. On one occasion he went so far as to bring a girl into the football locker room and carried her into the shower to have sex. I was there as it was happening. One of the boys reported immediately to the coach's room and said, "Come quickly to the locker room." Coach responded immediately and saved the girl from probable rape. They are out there and they are worldly.

This situation is not unique to men. Witness the cheerleaders who want to sleep with the entire football or basketball team. The unrighteous target the righteous to entrap them and bring them down to their level in the sewer. The impure will do their best to open and break through the walls that have been set up and then destroy. Since this is the modern era, think of the computer virus infecting every item of software with which it comes in touch. Even with security walls, we are tempted to find out what is in the message that seems so wonderful. Don't click on that message!

Imagine the shame of word getting around, as it inevitably does and usually from one of "them" that a person had sex. Now the road gets tougher to find the right girl or boy that can accept and forgive the incident or indiscretion.

What harmony is there between Christ and Belial (the devil)? Or what does a believer have in common with an unbeliever?"
II Cor. 6:15 (NIV)

I usually like the <u>New International Version</u> of the Bible and all quotes are from that version unless otherwise marked. The NIV translation of the Bible places the words in a modern language context. Paul asks us to think for ourselves. What indeed is there in common? The answer should be very little. Is that how you want to begin a relationship, begin dating, begin marriage, with very little in the emotional, mental, and spiritual piggybank? We can deal with little in the way of finances. True love makes up the difference. We can deal with little in the way of goods, or a place to live as long as righteous people have faith and have each other. Marriages often begin with little, but with vast potential. There is no potential with mental and spiritual bankruptcy.

Christ commanded us:

Therefore come out from them and be separate, says the Lord. Touch no unclean thing, and I will receive you."
II Cor. 6: 17 (NIV)

What a powerful command! Come out...Be separate....Touch no unclean thing...! How much clearer can I make these words about being unequally yoked? See the promise? "I will receive you." But wait. There is more and I relate it back to the yoking concept, as I believe I am led to do.

I will be a Father to you, and you will be my sons and daughters, says the Lord Almighty.
II Cor. 6:18 (NIV)

In other words, we are in a protected relationship. Paul might as well have said son-in-law and daughter-in-law. Equal matching means equal protection. A relationship built by the guidance of the Lord is the strongest relationship. I like to change old adages around. In this case let me ask, "When the going gets tough," Where are the tough?" The answer is the Lord provides the suit of armor and protection for body, soul, and spirit.

My Baptist Minister Uncle had it right in his sermons. As he expressed the change when a person becomes a Christian, "The 'Want

To' is changed." Equally matched, equally yoked Christians have the same "Want to." There is a meeting of the minds. Difficulties are overcome by common mutual prayer, not by "one pulling the load." Communication lines are open. Sharing problems is open. Discussions between unmarried boy and girl, and later between married spouses are illuminating and productive. Goals are commonly decided. Storm clouds give way to sunshine. Isn't that what everyone wants? Happiness?

I rather like the words of Amos 3:3. Although the prophet was not using his message in a man woman relationship way, the argument provides clarity to the thought process:

> ***Do two walk together unless they have agreed to?***
> ***Amos 3:3 (NIV)***

Great question! Certainly not in harmony unless there is agreement! They may be on the same road, but not walking together unless there is agreement. One may veer off on a side road that leads to perdition, while the other continues on the straight and narrow path unless they reinforce each other and together watch for the signs placed by the good and righteous.

The following is from the International Standard Version of the Bible.

> ***But just as then the son who was conceived***
> ***according to the flesh persecuted the son who was***
> ***conceived according to the Spirit, so it is now.***
> ***Galatians 4:29 (ISV)***

Wow! Read it again! "Persecuted!" Oh, those who are worldly, fleshly in their thinking and outlook, will persecute the ones conceived according to the Spirit The reference in the passage is to Ishmael, the fleshly one, who was born of Abraham's slave girl when Sarah felt Abraham had to have an heir and arranged the mating. Isaac was the son born to Sarah as God had promised. Do you understand how much conflict arose between the two? It persists to this day. Ishmael is commonly looked upon as the father of the Arabs, while Isaac was the father of the Israelites, although both go back to Abraham. Ishmael and Isaac was the split. How many centuries of conflict did that lead to? Now how about bottling that conflict up in one little marriage?

Isaac, the promised "after the promise" or chosen one, received injurious treatment from Ishmael "after the flesh". Paul in writing to the Corinthians was referring to Genesis 21:9, which says, *"Sarah saw the son of Hagar (Ishmael) the Egyptian, which she (Hagar) bore unto Abraham, mocking."* Because of this Sarah had Hagar and Ishmael expelled from the house of Abraham, according to Genesis 21:10. Sometimes the Christian has to expel the non-Christian, such as in severing a relationship.

If you have gained anything from this first chapter, it is looking for a positive Christian mate should be the first goal of the person starting to date and avoiding the fleshly "them" who are unequally matched from the start. The START is important. Of course there are no guarantees that the first person of the same faith a person dates is the one. Same faith people are not all pure in their thinking and it may take dating to reveal the inconsistencies in words and actions. Christians with Christians or Jews with Jews, however, are equally yoked at least by faith. There is a foundation on which to build a relationship. Equal matching of other characteristics remains to be seen and may be helped by reading the rest of the book. When there is a religious base there is the greatest likelihood that the person of the same faith selected for dating from the first time is the right one.

Suppose the other person one starts dating is not of the same faith. There is hope, but it is going to take some work to convert that person. Words and actions are needed. Do not be afraid to ask the relationship of the date partner with God. Better to ask one question than having to answer a thousand questions later. Tell the date partner you want him or her to come to church with you. Tell the person you are praying for him or her and their future. Show concern for the person's eternity. Give a Bible as a present. As you can see there are a lot of things that can be done, but the bottom line is the reaction of the other person. That will tell you all you need to know about continuing a relationship through to marriage.

The advice I am giving is heartfelt. The NIV Bible translation says: ***"Perfume and incense bring joy to the heart, and the pleasantness of a friend springs from their heartfelt advice."*** **(Proverbs 27:9)** Count me as a friend. Proverbs 22:3 provides the final piece of advice offered in this first chapter. The New Living Translation of the Bible has my preferred translation of this particular verse:

> ***A prudent person foresees the danger ahead***
> ***and takes precautions. The simpleton goes***
> ***blindly on and suffers the consequences.***
> ***Proverbs 22:3 (NLT)***

My Prayer for You: Let us all be prudent in foreseeing the danger ahead of not being equally yoked religiously at a minimum. Then let us take the precautions with our heart and future on the line to protect ourselves from pain, sorrow, and unhappiness. At least let us endeavor to find someone who completes us and believes as we do to raise the probability of success in marriage and happiness in life. Let us not be a blind fool who suffers the consequences even when the consequences are in plain view and we have been warned about them.

Chapter 2

Magnets and the Attraction Process

GOD PLACES US IN a pool of potential marriage partners. Finding the one that is the most right for us is the problem and the great unknown. The process is rather like a diamond miner selecting from stones that look like other stones, but there is something sparkly about this one. The problem for the one who buys the stone is not knowing what will be the cut, clarity, color, and carat (the four C's of buying an engagement ring, by the way) of the finished product. Even as a teenager, dating is the way to find the perfect, or at least best, fit for a future husband or wife. Initial physical attraction must be balanced against the more important features inside a person or that a person projects, such as confidence and maturity.

Magnets and Magnetism!! Comparing various studies as I have done for this book, there are some interesting differences in the lists of top ten qualities women want in a man and man wants in a woman that form the bases for initial and longer term attraction. In general, physical attributes rank near the top on the list of important qualities men look for in a woman while they rank near the bottom in the qualities that attract a woman. I will provide some general ideas for both men and women in things that attract them to the opposite sex using the terms "magnet" and "magnetism."

I started out to collect surveys of what attracts men to women and what attracts women to men. What I found was a cacophony of terms that provided general guidance, but not conclusive evidence. Each survey was conducted differently by age, culture, location, and race. There are some generalities that can be applied and a relative list of attributes or attractions, let's call them magnets, was produced. Age of the respondents matters in selection. The teenage girl is more likely to value looks and athletic ability in a boyfriend than a twenty something female.

Magnetism in Men

I like the word magnets. What attracts us to each other? Let us begin with what attracts women to men.

I will start with a sample from the Internet to show the inconsistencies and variations; however, when some of the words are combined, such as employment, own place, and owns car that equals independence. Affection, consideration, and thoughtfulness are really communication skills.

Magnet Men Attributes
for Women in Order According to Internet Sources

#	AskMen	Associated Content	Movie "Notebook"	Steven Aitchison
1	Confidence	Honesty	Confidence	Honesty
2	Ambition	Intelligence	Persistence	Protection
3	Sense of Humor	Smile	Faithfulness	Ambition
4	Passion	Sense of Humor	Keeps Promises	Support
5	Intelligence	Manners	Loving	Sense of Humore
6	Sociability	Sensitivity	Self Esteem	Reliability
7	Communication	Sincerity	Listen	Commitment
8	Positivity	Employed	Truth	Respect
9	Looks	Own Place	Realist	Sensitivity
10	Independence	Own Car	Commitment	Looks
11		Affectionate	Looks	Assertiveness
12		Considerate		Faithfulness

I obviously needed to make my own list. I like Top 10 lists, so I will stick with that, but what to put on the list and how to rank them. After careful consideration of these sources and psychological studies, I have come up with my own reasonable ranking of magnetism for women that they see in men. Some attributes in the above lists are combined into one larger category of magnetism.

The following chart is my own compilation of relative order for magnetism in men. I believe that the differences in the studies and sources depend on the population pool for the survey. My lists are oriented toward a man or woman looking for a mate and not a one-night stand. My list is very close to general reality.

Peterson Ranking of Magnetism in Men for Women Looking for a Marriage Partner

#	Magnet Category in Order
1	Confidence and Self Esteem (Voice/Demeanor)
2	Intelligence in one or more of nine categories
3	Honesty, Telling the Truth
4	Sense of Humor and Laugh at Oneself
5	Ambition, Dreams, Work Ethic
6	Caring
7	Faithfulness, Reliability, Dependability
8	Economic Prospects, Job, Inheritance
9	Looks
10	Independence

1. Confidence and Self Esteem

I am confident that "confidence" is the number one magnet that attracts a woman to a man. On almost every list besides the ones listed in the chart, Confidence Rules! Inherent in confidence is voice, demeanor, self esteem/self assurance, holding ones head high, and not being afraid to take chances.

Voice

A man's voice: pitch, tone, and modulation rate at the top of the list of magnets for women. Pitch is the primary attraction that women automatically sense in their internal evaluation (they are not even aware of it) genetic processing of who would make an ideal mate.

In an article dated July 18, 2008 and titled, "Voice and Attraction: What Effect Does Voice Pitch Have on Attractiveness " (101.com), John Connor reports on work done with a tribe in Tanzania regarding reproduction and attraction factors. The tribe was picked, since there are no sexual barriers and academically this reinforced the legitimacy of the findings, according to the author. The summation was "the deeper the voice the more potent and attractive the male." Professor Feinberg, McMaster University, Ontario, Canada, who conducted the study was quoted as saying "We think it's similar to a peacock's tail..." The tail doesn't help the peacock in the world, all it really does is attract females. In this case (men), it's testosterone that makes the voice more masculine at puberty." In the study 49 men and 52 women from the tribe were interviewed and recording made of the speaking about their reproductive history. "The frequency of pitch was noted and analysis showed men with deeper voices fathered more children. The deepest voiced man had 10 children...whereas the highest pitched had...three."

[Source: http://www.suite101.com/content/does-a-deep-voice-make-men-sexier-a59975]

In the same article a study conducted at Northumbria University in the United Kingdom confirmed the findings of Professor Feinberg. In the Northumbria study "Men and women were asked to rate the voices on things like attractiveness, dominance, confidence and sexiness... Both women and men rated deep voiced men more highly."

The ability to sing enhances a man's chances as well, but is much more important for the tenor voiced man than the bass voiced man. Deep strong voices that are well modulated when talking with a women or being listened to by a woman (on the phone, or in a room of people) trumps everything else as an initial attractor.

Self Esteem/Self Assurance

Women observe how a man sits, stands, and walks (unconsciously) as an assessment of self assurance and confidence. Arrogance is a repelling force, but confidence trumps physical appearance. An Ezine Article titled, "The 4 Traits of a Sexually Desirable Man," stated that "Women are naturally drawn to confident men because they make them feel safe." The author made the comment, "A self-assured manner is so much more attractive than a mouse of a man who looks skittish, nervous and ready to run."

[Source: http://ezinearticles.com/?The-4-Traits-of-an-Sexually-Desirable-Man&id=555934]

Risk Taker

A confident person is a risk taker and fits in the "Alpha" male category knowing that risk brings reward. Women are attracted to speed, endurance, danger, and the dark side at least initially. Risk is not recklessness though, and women still want to feel safe.

Eye Contact

A confident man makes the right amount of eye contact with a woman. Too little eye contact makes a man seem disinterested or evasive. Staring on the other hand can make a man seem intimidating and a potential stalker. From the same Ezine article there is a good number to think about, "A man who keeps his eyes on the woman he is talking to about 80% of the time will come across as being interested and seem attractive to her.

[Source: http://ezinearticles.com/?The-4-Traits-of-an-Sexually-Desirable-Man&id=555934]

Persistence as a Confidence Technique

I will include "Persistence" (as mentioned in the third column in second place) as being generated by confidence. A persistent man is a confident man, or at least communicating that trait. Never underestimate persistence. Most of us do. Persistence is not trying just to get one's way, but is remaining focused on the goal in a loving way. After that, following another person, invading their territory on a regular basis, or confronting them is stalking and stalkers win restraining orders. Sending notes over time, reconnecting after a month or so, not being afraid to send a small gift can signal persistence and a strong person that can take rejection and keep on plugging.

For a portrayal of persistence I recommend seeing the movie, "The Notebook." This is becoming a modern classic. Ryan Gosling plays the young Noah and Rachel McAdams is the young Allie. Allie lives in the city and comes from wealth. Noah does not have enough money to buy a candy bar. They meet, fall in love, and then Allie's mom squashes the romance, or so she believes by sending Allie off to private school and out of Noah's reach. After seven years Allie returns to where she met Noah and must choose between her wealthy fiancée and Noah, who has progressed, but obviously not made a fortune. Seven years of unrequited love and Noah persists! A tear please. A quote from one of the letters being read is:

"I am no one special; just a common man with common thoughts, and I've led a common life. There are no monuments dedicated to me and my name will soon be forgotten. But in one respect I have succeeded as gloriously as anyone who's ever lived: I've loved another with all my heart and soul; and to me, this has always been enough."

2. Intelligence

The second magnet for women is intelligence. In the combined discussion later in Chapter 3, I will present the nine types of intelligence a good number of psychologists accept today in place of the older one dimensional test. Men and women do have differences in some of the intelligence measurements and by the year 2011, biologists have finally come around to accepting the differences based on women having slightly larger lobes for some tasks and men for others. Spatial intelligence is more likely to be higher in a male for example than in a female, while a female exhibits earlier vocabulary development.

How intelligence is demonstrated and used is as important as having the sets of intelligence to be discussed. A quiet use of intelligence to resolve problems, do homework, and achieve results in tasks set by us and for us is admired. The loudmouth braggart that is always calling attention to himself or herself and saying in effect look at me, is a turn off.

3. Honesty

Magnet number three is honesty. This is not an initial attraction, since it has to be demonstrated in a situation first, but it is consistently at or near the top of things women admire in a man, so I have placed it here. Honesty does not mean to be untactful in some situations. A woman asks the opinion of a man, "Does this dress make me look fat?" The man really has no clue how to approach this question. "You are fat in any dress," may be honest, but I hope you have a doghouse for the night in which to sleep.

"You are so beautiful, who cares what the dress looks like," will net you positive points and endear you to her. Besides she is probably the only person wondering if a dress makes her look fat.

She may also be on a fishing expedition to find out if you still love her of all things. The older the woman becomes the more trap quiz questions you will have to face. By then honesty is not only the best policy, it is the only one. Your woman will respect you and your opinion as long as it is honest, but do not jump into the traps. You can be honest without hurting feelings or the relationship.

4. Sense of Humor

On three of the scales that I found, sense of humor comes in at numbers three, four, and five. I figure number four is the golden mean. We are not just talking about making jokes or taking a joke gracefully from someone else pulled on us, but rather the ability to laugh even under stressful conditions and find the comical in the irretrievable. As mentioned in Wikibooks.org, "Laughing connects your limbic brain and cerebral cortex, enabling better awareness of your emotions."

[Source: http://en.wikibooks.org/wiki/Relationships/ How_Women_Select_Men]

Now there's a mouthful. What it really means is that by laughing we are reducing not only our own tension, but that of those around us. Furthermore, the innocent well-phrased twist of words can have healing effects on another person. I found a note on a social website that said, "I cannot find any pants to fit me because I am too tall." My response was "You are vertically challenged, now here are two place on the Internet to purchase your size pants." The person wrote back, "That is soooo funny!!!"

Buffoons and clowns are not magnets. Juvenile humor is for the guys and stag parties. You do not have to be the life of the party, just one who laughs at good jokes and enjoys sprinkling in witty sayings you have learned or appropriate stories and quotes that can fascinate besides reveal one of the forms of intelligence.

5. Ambition

AskMen.com lists ambition second and Steven Aitchison lists ambition third in the order of "magnets", so I suppose I need to insert it by now. One list leaves it out and on one list I can equate it to being gainfully employed in eighth place. I am going to incorporate into ambition the concept of serious dreams about what a man wants to be in five or ten years, or even longer. The ambitious man is the focused man in whatever field he chooses, from being a farmer to being an astronaut.

Demonstrating the ability to work at an early age, taking summer jobs, planning for a future career, or focusing on just a few skill areas are ways to demonstrate ambition. Beyond that it is a promise. My ambition was to be a lawyer, but I never had the money to go to law school. Instead I became an Army Officer and my wife occasionally brought up the fact that one of her reasons for marrying me was my promise to be a lawyer.

Success at work is a better magnet than money and earns respect. What attracts women is the discipline they see in a man, his strong work ethic regardless of status job, and commitment and dedication to a task or tasks to accomplish something. The paycheck is often the measuring stick, but discerning women, and there are a majority of them, see the work, any work, as progress toward a goal and will support that goal.

If money, success, and business sense were the greatest measures, Warren Buffet would be the top magnet, but there are other things that are important to attracting women. In this category women want ambition of any kind and respect the man willing to present his ambitions and share his dreams.

6. Caring

Somewhere amalgamating the terms of passion, sensitivity, communication, supportive, loving, and affectionate is the term "caring." I need all those words to blend into caring. A caring person is passionate, driven by caring, sensitively conditioned by caring, communicative with a woman because he cares, supportive of her in any situation because he cares for her and her feelings, and loving her and the essence of her.

Passion is one component of caring. Women love passion in a man. Witness the "passionate" affairs. Passion is not only on display in the bedroom, but women love the fact a man is serious about something good and decent and productive. A passion for one's religious beliefs is the best passion a man can have. It takes in devotion, love, commitment, adventure, and excitement. The reason women are more likely to join in humanitarian efforts is because they are more nurturing. But having men join in a "cause" is exciting and adventurous. A woman may find it hard to understand the passion for a football team, but does understand the passion for something she can share. Philanthropy is sexy, but don't give away the family nest egg.

Sensitivity is another component of caring. Sensitivity shows that you are paying attention, listening to the female problems and opinions, and can be gentle. Some sources I read have it all wrong. I hate the term "get in touch with your feminine side." It sounds like someone is ready to cross-dress and pretend to be a woman. A caring man will not be afraid to show tenderness, speak in a soft soothing tone, hold the girl or woman who is pouring out her feelings let alone her tears, and at least try to understand what is going on in her life. Women find this approach manly, not anti-macho. For some men this is not a natural thing in the beginning, but the change happens with true love and caring for the other person.

Communicative: Never shut the door on *communication*. This is a tough one for men. Men internalize their feelings, their problems, their perceived failures. Women lay them out on the table for inspection by whosoever passes by the table. Listening is the most underrated communication skill. A good listener is an active listener. That means paying attention and inserting a minor comment here and there, asking a simple question, or making a positive interjection. You don't have to have the solution. In fact it would probably be rejected anyway.

Women place a priority on a guy who will listen attentively and can express themselves in a wise way. The Bible is a good place to turn for a quote or a proverb to help out. Women need to be aware that men are action-oriented. Men are ready to pick a fight to solve the problem. Many a fight has unintentionally been started by a woman opening up and discussing things that would cause a man to take action. Men believe that there has to be a solution, some action necessary to take care of the situation, some key to the door. Women aren't looking for a solution—necessarily. The man usually asks, hopefully to himself only, if there is not some action goal why talk?

Supportive: The *supportive* component again is not an action thing, but it may require being assertive on behalf of a girlfriend or spouse to let them know you care. It is positively indicating acceptance of the woman's point of view (legal and moral of course), making little suggestions such as why not try this, and standing up for her in a crowd.

I wonder how many western movies I have seen where the man fails to be assertive and the girlfriend rides off with another man?

Love and Affection are last on my list of caring items, but are the most important. They are the strongest forms of caring. Love overcomes, affection sustains. I discuss love in the love chapter of this book, but a word about caring. Caring is the result of a deep and abiding love. Love overcomes time and distance, the partner who strays into an affair or more, and yet love is patient and strong.

Affection is both physical and mental. It is a mental state of being that softens men and wilts the heart. Affection is a component of physical sex including kissing and caressing. Affection leads to thoughtfulness and being considerate.

Touching is part of affection. Put your hand on her arm or wrist while talking. Hold her hand for no reason. Massage her back or rub her feet. The results will be amazing.

7. Faithfulness, Reliability, Promise Keeping, Dependability

A few years ago Promise Keepers was a major crusade in support of the family and home. Men became Promise Keepers and the affect on home life was dramatic. I can only imagine the pride and affection in the hearts of wives and mothers of Promise Keepers.

I had to deploy three terms here for essentially one idea magnet and that is standing like a century old tree with roots in the ground. Is there a word for that? Steadfast, secure, unwavering, always there, protecting? The man that does one does all three. The faithful man is the reliable man is the promise keeper. How is that for a rationalist tautology? A woman wants someone on whom she can depend. Dependability must be added.

Faithfulness is easy to define in a relationship. Don't go with another woman, don't commit adultery, and don't even take a chance that a situation can be misunderstood. Get out of there. There is absolutely no excuse for not remaining faithful and the consequences are dire. The Bible teaches that the wages of sin is death. Is that strong enough?

Reliability is always being somewhere as close to time as possible. A girl/woman must know you can be counted on to do things important to her as well as the relationship. Of course the woman understands work and overtime, but how many times can overtime be an excuse without suspicions being generated? If the girlfriend has told her family you are coming over for a meal and you do not show up, call, or deliver an excuse, short of death and the hospital, you better have a powerful verifiable reason. Getting drunk with the boys is not one of them.

Promise Keeping is easy to list hard to perform. Forgetting to do something does not provide a reason in the mind of your girlfriend or woman. A promise is a promise is a promise. Promise keepers persist in the effort to fulfill a promise they have made.

Dependability means always being available emotionally and physically if necessary. Even when a husband is deployed in the military overseas, being available emotionally by letter or the opportunity to call home is important to a woman.

A woman needs to know you are there for her in sickness and in health. You will take a cold sponge to her fevered brow. You will buy the cold medicine to make things better. You will leave your job to take care of an urgent matter, not to you, but to her.

8. Economic Prospects

Economics prospects differ from ambition. What are the goals the man has in mind? How big does he want to grow a business? How much does he need to invest? When can he obtain a positive cash flow and when can he support a family? These are not the dreams of ambition, but the reality of producing money, paying the mortgage, paying for food and the car and the gas needed to get to work and school.

9. Looks

I warned you about looks. They are way down the list of magnets, although it doesn't hurt to have nice looks and a well toned body. Women appreciate that as part of the total package. I will discuss physical attributes in a combined way shortly, but here being clean, neat, well groomed, and smelling good actually improve looks. "Smelling good" improves looks? Yes, because it changes perceptions.

Women don't ask for a lot on the looks scale. Men, if it is in the top ten on any list, it is still important. Despite the hair on chests and back, more sharply defined angles than the gentle curves of a woman, often unruly hair, and skin made of sandpaper, women still are interested. Enhancing looks is important for every man, but more so for the lesser 25%. Clothes that look nice and fit properly, staying in some semblance of shape, and brushing teeth and hair are not too much to ask.

10. Independence

Making decisions, cooking a meal, operating in the woods, or fishing are all signs of the independent man. Women want to know that a man can take care of himself and then turn around and want to take care of him and strip him of his independence. Go figure. No woman wants to be your mother, except your mother. A guy who is in constant need of reassurance, approval, advice from others on how to do things, and fears to do things is a guy that quickly will be by himself if not already.

The Magnet Woman

The magnet girl/woman has a very different profile. From a combination of sources, some advice from a girl, some from psychological studies, some from observations, and some from lists. Men are rational and visual, so the order of things changes. As with a woman being attracted to a man, there is someone for everyone.

Peterson Rank Magnetism of Women for Men Looking for a Marriage Partner

	Magnet Category in Order
1	Looks (Face, Physical Structure, Femininity)
2	Modesty for Wife/Immodesty for Fling
3	Confidence (Way of Walking, Demeanor)
4	Sense of Humor and Laugh at Oneself
5	Voice
6	Kindness, Gentleness, Soft heartedness
7	Intelligence in at least one of nine categories
8	Love and Affection
9	Character and Reputation
10	Homemaking Skills (Marriage Suitability)

1. Looks

Looks run the gamut from physical structure to femininity. Men are attracted to all the physical features and shapes of a woman. Body shape is surprisingly less high on the list of looks than women presume. Breast size is just not that important as Playboy and other magazines think they are. Breasts come in all shapes and sizes, each shape and size fascinating.

Let's cover the major traits of interest to a male. Hair is probably the first thing a boy/man sees in focus. That is why men are so disappointed when men wear long hair. Second is body shape including legs, torso, ratio and proportion of hips, thighs, stomach, waist, and breasts. These magnets pull in the eyes of the male to focus on femininity, dress, eyes, lips, and smile.

Hair: Most men start with an appraisal of a woman with the length of her hair and most are magnetized by shoulder length hair, or hair somewhere in the vicinity. A lot of men think a young short haired woman is not feminine and would make an unsuitable partner. Shoulder length hair maximizes the number of "hits" by the opposite sex. Color is genetically determined, but women find changing their visible hair color to be something else will be a magnet to a larger range of the male population. Since blondes are the exception in most societies, blondes really do have more fun. Guess which shades of hair dye are the most popular in sales.

Body Shape: Everything in proportion—weight, height, curves, legs, torso, breasts, neck, and face. Another feature of shoulder length hair is it hides the ears, which is often a good thing. Breasts and derriere are the least important of the body features on sight. The most important is the waist to hip ratio. Leg shape is more important than breasts. Muscle tone can be determined by the legs along with slenderness of the ankles and soft undulation of the calf muscles.

Femininity and Dress: Men want women that look feminine with finely defined facial features and curves that can be seen and not deduced. Feminine dresses emphasize the curves and enhance magnetism. Hair plays a part in appearing feminine, which is why the shoulder length hair is seen as more attractive. Femininity is a trait men lack and so it is exciting to them to see feminine women.

Eyes: Women have obsessed forever about improving the eyes and the immediate area around the eyes. Products such as eyeliner and mascara are multi-million dollar sellers. It works. Other than that, there are some cultural features about the color of the iris. In ancient China and across the Mongol Empire, green eyes were treasured and when a girl was found with "jade green" eyes, she was often delivered to the emperors for their harem. Beyond that, men are attracted to eyes of all colors, so don't worry about colored contacts.

Eye shape is cultural and there are differing interpretations of eye shape. There is no reason for Asian girls with almond shaped eyes to attempt to become "round eyes." Eyes speak volumes to a man especially when locking on to each other with eye to eye contact and observing expressions. Pupil dilation at excitement is subconsciously communicated to the man and in turn excites him. Some men simply fall in love with a woman's eyes.

Lips, Mouth, Smile: The smile of a woman can melt the heart of a beast. Subconsciously men are attracted by the lips and mouth as much as the smile. Lipstick does enhance a man's desire and color sends separate signals. The color red is associated with "hot" and is the color best suited for attracting a male.

There have been few studies about the affect of color on psychology. Researchers at the University of Rochester in 2008 published an article in the Journal of Personality and Social Psychology explaining the results of testing the color red as a perception and trigger for the interest of men. Red is cross-cultural from the red ochre paint tribal women use to the "Red Light Districts," associated with prostitutes and sex. Red also is a status color in some countries much as purple was in the Bible.

In the Rochester study, five experiments were conducted demonstrating that the color "red" is the most magnetic color for men and they are not even aware. Researchers claim this is the first empirical study that documents scientifically the effects of color on behavior patterns, which is surprising considering all the clothing, facial cosmetic, and lipstick companies out there. According to Elliott, much is known about the physics and physiology of color, but not the psychology. The researchers argue men's response is not the product of societal conditioning, but of deep rooted primal roots. According to the study,

"Under all of the conditions, the women shown framed by or wearing red were rated significantly more attractive and sexually desirable by men than the exact same women shown with other colors. When wearing red, the woman was also more likely to score an invitation to the prom and to be treated to a more expensive outing.

"The red effect extends only to males and only to perceptions of attractiveness. Red did not increase attractiveness ratings for females rating other females and red did not change how men rated the women in the photographs in terms of likability, intelligence or kindness.

"Although red enhances positive feelings in this study, earlier research suggests the meaning of a color depends on its context. For example, Elliot and others have shown that seeing red in competition situations, such as written examinations or sporting events, leads to worse performance.

"The current findings have clear implications for the dating game, the fashion industry, product design and marketing."

[Source: Source: Elliot, A. J., & Niesta, D. (2008). Romantic red: Red enhances men's attraction to women. *Journal of Personality and Social Psychology, 95,* 1150–1164.]

Skin Tone: Guess what? The cosmetic companies are right. Skin tone, not just color of skin, but tone of the skin, acts as a magnet to men's eyes. Skin tone does not mean turning everyone brown. What it does mean is a healthy glow of the skin attracts the eyes of men. A little red added to skin tone on the face may be all that is needed to heighten the appeal.

2. Modesty v. Immodesty

What the woman is trying to accomplish with dress and color plays a role in the dating and relationship game. Men will chase both the modest girl and the immodest looking woman, but want to marry the modest.   Men lust for the immodest, generally speaking and fall in love with the modest. An immodestly dressed woman will be perceived to be a one night stand. "Hot" immodest women are viewed by men as high maintenance, sharing charms with everyone, and less reliable.

A chastely dressed girl will attract men looking for a wife as well as the serial seducer. What men want in their long term relationship is a woman who acts modestly in mixed company, dresses modestly for parties or events, and talks modestly without sexual innuendo or flirting with others. I'm not talking bashful, or wallflower, or an act. I am talking conduct. For a long term relationship men want a woman they can take home to their mother.

3. Confidence

"The walk" demonstrates confidence. That is why in the past mothers made their daughters put books on their head and practice walking fluidly without dropping the books. Posture is a component of confidence with the straight standing and walking girl being perceived as confident and the slouch as not having much.

Confidence is more than walking and standing. Confidence is also understanding one's own strengths and weakness and working to improve in all facets of life. Having a Christian or Jewish perspective and attending Sunday School and church services or synagogue also brings a quiet peace and confidence to the mind and soul. Men feel good around a woman who manifests a sense of inner confidence and can feel at home and make the man feel comfortable in any dating environment.

4. Sense of Humor

There is something about the high pitched laugh of a tickled woman that endears her to a man. Humor can be found in any situation. A woman who can see, understand, and express that humor is a magnet. The same things said under paragraph 4 in magnets of women to men apply here. Do not hesitate to express disapproval for off-color jokes. Expressing disapproval actually puts the man in a deficit status where he feels he needs to make it up to you. You can also gauge a man's friends and thought processes by the jokes he tells and how he laughs at them when presented.

Make sure to laugh only at funny things and not sensitivities of the man. A laugh can be an insult or it can be an ego booster. The situation will dictate. Just be aware.

5. Voice

The thrill of a soaring soprano voice, the soft dulcet tones of the contralto, the husky smoky allure of the alto, attract different men. Voice was not discussed where women being attracted to men were concerned; however, I am betting if I had presented the top twenty magnets voice to a man voice would rank between 11 and 15 on the list.

A man's voice can seduce a woman. A woman's voice can do the same thing. One of the reasons for Marilyn Monroe's success was not only her physical allure, but her bedroom voice. The smoky blues songs of Julie London back in the 1950's drove a lot of men crazy. Listen to "Cry me a River" on YouTube and see what I mean.

6. Kindness and Soft Heartedness

Some bloggers think kindness and soft heartedness is the "most likely" trait to attract a man, but I did not find any studies suggesting that. The soft side is part of the femininity equation as well. Women look to their fathers for models for their boyfriends. Men look to their mothers for models of their ideal mate for life. Even if a mother has been cold to her children, they still seek warmth, soothing words, kind displays of affection, and words that bring comfort.

Women often complain that they don't want a mother's boy as a boyfriend, but men tend to fall for the woman who offers them a viable substitute. Why not display the softness and warmth?

7. Intelligence

Men often fall for the waitress that warmly greets them and brings them their morning coffee and eggs. That tells you a lot about men and why I have ranked intelligence lower on my list of magnets. Don't get me wrong. We are still dealing with the top 10 list here, but unless we are comparing IQ's for a mate, men probably do not know the level of intelligence of the woman, but suspect it from conversation, achievement, and grades. As with any magnet, more is better, but the display of it is crucial.

Acting stupid or saying dumb things does not endear a man to a woman, but turns his attentions elsewhere. You are free to look ahead to the nine forms of intelligence and evaluate them for yourself.

8. Love and Affection

Love and affection are different from kindness and soft heartedness. Now we are back in the realm of caring and being oriented on the other potential mate. Going back to the previous discussion under Caring, love overcomes, affection is sustaining. Touching the others hand, shoulder, arm are all part of love and affection. Words are important including the simple, "I love you," that can never be said often enough.

9. Strength of Character

Reputation is easy to destroy and hard to maintain. One little slip and a woman becomes branded. Men do want a woman who demonstrates integrity, is strong for them under most conditions, and can be trusted with secrets. The strength of character woman is supportive of the man to all comers, friends and foe alike. In Chapter 8, I will discuss the absolute fundamental of support for each other in public and building up the other when out with friends and relatives.

10. Homemaking Skills

The Pillsbury commercial got it right. "Nothing says lovin' like something from the oven." There is an old expression, "The way to a man's heart is through his stomach." Go back to the model mother. She cooked, sewed, cleaned up, did the washing, ironed the clothes, vacuumed the house, cleaned the blinds, and cared for the children. This model is still alluring to a man, particularly the cooking part. Men get a warm feeling passed on from their mothers when a woman they love feeds them with something homemade. Cooking a breakfast, evening meal, or even just bringing a pumpkin pie can turn a man to jelly. Sorry about the food pun.

In modern western society some of those things have been taken over by a maid, housekeeper, and baby sitter. Work schedule to make ends meet where the wife and husband are both working to earn money, has meant a sharing of tasks. What woman does not like to have the husband take over grilling meals on the weekend? What man will refuse to help around the house? Still the ideal persists and the woman who can demonstrate homemaking skills stands a superior chance of not just attracting the male, but "having him eating out of her hand." Giving a man homemade cookies and pumpkin pie is enough to keep him coming back for more.

Just as there is a man for every woman, there is a woman for every man. Your goal is to find the one that best satisfies you and your needs.

Chapter 3

Magnets at Work: Putting it Together

Physical Attributes of Men and Women

Men: As I presented in Chapter 2, the good news is being handsome and muscular rates low for women. The muscular structure of men is very different, as of course is women's. Some men develop large biceps and chests or power muscles, while other men have longer muscles that may be just as powerful and usually mean faster twitch muscles for running and quick strikes. Consider the differences between images of Hercules from a short wide statue in stone to a more lithe bronze statue in Italy. Surprisingly women prefer men that are leaner and yet are strong than the beefy men with large bicep muscles.

Women: Your looks are highly important for men, but the good news is different looks attract different men. The eyes of each person perceive a different idea of beauty. That means everyone is attractive to someone. General cultural images of beauty and handsomeness vary and changes over time. Look at the art of 500 years ago, or even a hundred years ago.

Big bodied women with plus sizes were the image of beauty such as can be seen in the paintings of Rubens. The term "reubenesque" comes from the preferences of Rubens in women.

Rubens, Venus at the Mirror

The ancient Greeks had a more slender figure of Venus in mind. Rather than displaying the Venus de Milo with arms broken off, I prefer the Venus painting as shown below:

As one can see, the images of beauty change and we have not even considered racial differences and preferences.

Stature for Men

In surveys, the height of a man does matter. Most women want their man to be taller as a minimum. Perhaps it makes them feel protected to be in their shadow.

"In surveys, most women stated the desired height of their mate should be six feet (182.88 cm). Interestingly, the average US male height is 5 feet 9 inches (175.26 cm). Improved body posture can increase height and also signals self-confidence. (Guys, suck in your gut, too.)"

http://www.master-your-dating-tips.com/modern-women-want. html

Intelligence

Intellectual capability is important for functioning in society, but is not as important as some other factors in establishing a romantic relationship. Witness the straight A girl going for the physical strength of the football captain who may or may not exhibit intelligence. Psychologists have found that there are various forms of intelligence.

The concept of multiple intelligences was defined by Howard Gardner in 1983 to describe and explain why cognitive processes and different abilities exist. Intelligence is a complex set of variables with each person on earth having more or less of the forms of intelligence presented by Gardner. Howard Gardner presented nine forms of intelligence:

1. Spatial:

Ability to visualize space.

2. Linguistic:

Ability to learn a language or languages and understand literal and figurative meanings of words.

3. Logical-mathematical:

Ability to deal with logic, abstractions, reasoning, and numbers. This correlates with traditional views of IQ testing. This is a good place to insert one example of why the logical-mathematical paradigm for intelligence was flawed. As Howard Gardner points out:

"...the theory states that a child who learns to multiply easily is not necessarily more intelligent than a child who has stronger skills in another *kind* of intelligence. The child who takes more time to master simple multiplication 1) may best learn to multiply through a different approach, 2) may excel in a field outside of mathematics, or 3) may even be looking at and understand the multiplication process at a fundamentally deeper level. Such a fundamentally deeper understanding can result in what looks like slowness and can hide a mathematical intelligence potentially higher than that of a child who quickly memorizes the multiplication table despite a less detailed understanding of the process of multiplication."

[Source: Wikipedia]

4. Bodily-kinesthetic:
Body control and skillful handling of objects.

5. Musical:
Sensitivity to sounds, rhythms, tones, and music. Musical ability often correlates with high linguistic skills.

6. Interpersonal:
Usually extroverts with good communication skills including ability to work in a group and sensitivity to moods, feelings, temperaments, and motivations.

7. Intrapersonal:
Usually introverts who are intuitive, self-reflective, and understand themselves.

8. Naturalistic:
Adaptability and relating to ones surroundings and the environment.

9. Existential:
Ability to comprehend philosophical concepts and phenomena or data beyond sensory data.

[Source: Howard Gardner. Frames of Mind: The Theory of Multiple Intelligences. New York: Basic Books, 1983.]

I am tempted to make a chart showing the nine forms of intelligence as defined by Gardner and then on the opposing axis place percentages by tens, but I fear another book would be required in order to define the percentages. Each person has some percentage of each of the forms of intelligence whether it is 10% or 100%, plus adding them up would reach 900% for the person that has all of them at a high level, though I suspect one does not exist at 900%.

There is usefulness, however, in thinking about one's own intelligence patterns and how they fit with a partner for life.

Emotional Stability and Personality Development

Emotional stability and personality development are somewhat aligned in that they determine how far we are from our own ideal and how far we perceive another person to be from our ideal. Emotional stability is somewhat difficult to measure, but it does communicate maturity, good upbringing, and educational sources including Sunday School and church. Loud outbursts, threats to others, and treatment of women are important clues to emotional stability or instability.

Personality matrices have been developed for comparative purposes. One that can be found on the Internet is the Advanced Multidimensional Personality Matrix (AMPM) that uses a series of questions to provide an assessment of personality types. The AMPM uses almost 300 questions to provide a self-assessment. The AMPM has five major classifications including emotional stability and measures 37 distinct personality traits. The self-assessment tells you who you are and how it is aligned with your ideal personality, what you want to be. Results can be used to increase personal satisfaction and improve chances for success in life. The five primary assessment scales used in this case are:

1. Emotional Stability versus Emotional Instability

2. Extraversion versus Introversion

3. Openness versus Closed Type

4. Agreeableness versus Disagreeableness

5. Conscientiousness versus Not Being Conscientious

Personality style impacts motivations, behavior, relationships, maturity level and has a causal effect on how a person reacts to challenges and stress.

[Source: http://www.queendom.com/tests/apops/ampm_r.html]

Work Capacity

How much work does the partner do. Homework study, after hours jobs, athletic drive, summer jobs, and full time jobs are indicators of future work and responsibility quotients. Some people have an infinite capacity for putting their nose to the grindstone, while others seem to have an infinite capacity for play. Sports is defined as work, since it requires discipline, attendance, taking instructions, working with a team, leadership traits, and other social enculturation.

Study does not measure the grade and the grade does not measure the work. For many with a particular type of intelligence, limited study is required, while for another study may entail hard work, taking notes, and difficulty in completing homework. What I am saying is this is a difficult variable to measure and consider in the dating process. Cheating, however, is a measure that affects not only those around the cheater, but robs society of disciplined leaders. Here are some thoughts on work capacity:

1. Multitasking:

Does the person do all things well and take on a larger share of all activity and job related preparation?

2. Homework:

Does the person do their own homework? Do they have good grades as result? Have you seen the other person in a study situation, such as study hall or up close and personal in a study group or with you?

3. Jobs:

Does the other person take on leadership jobs in high school or college such as decorating a float, playing a musical instrument, or earning extra money? I define jobs as not just ones paying a salary or wage, but as extracurricular activities not formally classified as jobs, but requiring the same things as sports, i.e. attendance, discipline, working with others.

4. Athletic Drive or Learning to Play a Musical Instrument:

Playing a sport is not essential for those that have difficulty in athletic endeavors, but athletic drive, as opposed to just playing a sport) is a characteristic of a hard working person who is striving to become the best they can be. Even a third-stringer may be putting forth maximum effort and just not have the physical talent to succeed. Commitment to tasks and desire to improve are difficult to measure by athletic success, but the very fact of playing a sport increases the chances of a person learning to work hard, endure hardships, and overcome obstacles.

Learning to play a musical instrument, by the way, is a significant attraction for women. Even learning the basics and being able to play one song improves the perception of intellectual abilities.

Economic Prospects

Surprisingly economic prospects are hard to predict and are less important than people imagine. The person that seems incapable of any future economic security may be the inventor or entrepreneur that is the next billionaire, while a person in a rich family may lose the family fortune.

Dreams and goal setting come into play as far as economic prospects, but there is more to it than that. Willingness to do any job or task is equally important to determining whether a person can provide for a family. Notice I used the word person and boy or girl. In modern society it is not necessary that the man be the dominant money earner.

During the great depression, states passed laws that if a man was a wage earner, farmer, or the like, the woman could not take a job outside the home, since it would deprive another family of wages. When my mother was applying for a teaching job in South Dakota, she was asked if she was married and if so, did her husband make money in any fashion? My mother was indeed single, so she was hired by the school board to teach.

After World War II, my own family situation was that my mother was the dominant wage earner throughout life and my father was secondary. That did not mean my father did not work or did not have dreams. My father in fact returned as a soldier from the war and my mom and dad set about buying a farm and the equipment necessary to farm with money earned by my mother and made payments from her salary. The farm was not highly productive because of the soil and crop rotation meant the higher selling corn and oats had to give way to a year of planting alfalfa to restore the nitrogen in the soil. This was supplemented by manure from the cow barn.

Dad was committed to farming. During the war he was an aircraft mechanic on the P=-51 Mustang, the most advanced fighter of the time. Everyone encouraged him to go to Chicago and work for his uncle, who was a vice-president of United Airlines, or work on a military base, but my dad was steadfast in working to fulfill his dream of being a farmer. Dad took additional jobs like umpiring and refereeing sports for $5 a game, selling seed corn in an already saturated seed corn market, selling Oliver farm equipment, buying a poor little gas station in a poor location in town, and providing janitorial service for churches and schools.

Finally concluding that they would need money to send me to college, my mother found a teaching job in West Texas and my family moved. Dad had no job, but the teaching job paid three times the South Dakota pay scale. Dad started working as the church janitor and hauling 100 pound sacks of mud to oil drilling sites. Hard work again and low pay, but a contribution to the family finances nevertheless. In later years, my dad worked as the high school janitor and always ran the clock at sporting events and umpired Little League baseball. Additionally, my dad became the town handyman and was called to paint houses, roof houses and churches, and fix things all at $2 an hour in the 1980's. These were not financially rewarding jobs, but work was important to him and no one worked harder. I assisted by working summer jobs in high school, getting two scholarships in college and working part time in college reducing the burden of my parents. My mother and father retired in their home that had been purchased in the 1950s and was paid. With their combined retirement they had sufficiency to travel to Europe, take annual trips back to South Dakota for family reunions and were extremely happy together.

The point is finances are shared in marriage and the man does not have to be the dominant wage earner. In fact in the economy of 2011, when this book is being written, the highest number of layoffs of men since the Great Depression is placing financial strain on a vast number of families. The family that shares finances, however, earned and can adjust to changing economic conditions will survive and be all the better for it.

Love, sharing, caring and leading a Christ filled life are more important than money. An inexpensive vacation at the beach or in the mountains may be as romantic as taking off for Tahiti. The boy/man should never feel guilty about making less money. After all, in marriage, joint decisions are made about the use of money, budgeting, planning for retirement, vacations and their cost, insurance, and medical plans. Money is treated equally 50/50.

I remember consulting with a young couple (actually just the girl) at the University of Arizona that had gotten married while still in college. I was a graduate teaching assistant working on my doctorate. She approached me after a lecture and asked my opinion on the use of money by her husband in "her" bank account. She came from a financially well-off family. I asked, "What do you feel is the problem?" She answered, "When I got married, I had my account and he had his." My husband wants us to put all our money together, but I have a lot and he does not have much. I want him to go out and make more money and then we can open a joint account." I asked, "Did you marry for love?" She looked at me with pupils dilated. "I married for love and future prospects of him taking care of me." I asked, "How rich is your family?" She said the approximate number. I asked, "Do you think he can ever earn that much money alone?" She responded with a drawn out, "Noooo." I told her the choices were very simple. "In marriage money is pooled together and shared regardless of source?" If there is love, that source, unless of course it is illegal, does not matter and it should not matter who contributed the most." The last I heard they were still married.

An old saying is "All work and no play makes Jack a dull boy." I rephrased it to read, "All work and no play makes jack," the term "jack" being an old slang expression for money. There must be some time in a premarital relationship and in marriage for togetherness, for romantic interludes, for playing together, but work to earn money is more important. Quality time together in a premarital relationship is also more important than daily "seeing" each other. Make those quality times count.

A final note on economic prospects: A woman considers not just her position, but that of her offspring. She needs to know that the man can support the whole family and that he will share his resources with his family to the point of depriving himself of his own desires. Women will run from men who cannot survive on their own, do not have an independent source of income and who are dominated by peers.

Status is one clue for a woman, but for young girls, status is hard to understand. Of course social standing at school becomes relevant and a gauge of popularity of boys with the girls. Parents will know social status and communicate it to their sons and daughters. Thus over a year or two perceptions become changed and conditioned by parents. Status is associated for parents not with popularity or success on a sports field, but with resources commanded by parents and the social standing those resources indicate.

In most cases older men are able to marshal more resources than a young boy. Older men are also attracted to younger women and compete with the boy for their affections. Women on the other hand are looking for dependability, reliability, and stability and are much less likely to go down in age until their middle life, when they are seeking approval anywhere they can get it and then it is not for a mate, but for an affair. Older women do hate younger women, because they see them as a threat and rightly so.

According to a website titled Master-your-dating-tips,

"Even after the childbearing years are over, men and women don't change their preferences for a mate. Women's preferences for a man stay relatively the same at any age. At the top of men's list of preferences for a woman is usually that she be young, good looking, and sexy - no matter what his age is. That is what worked in ancient times for men to make the healthiest DNA packages (i.e. his offspring). It seems that the software that drives the internal unconscious mental "computer" for mate selection does not come with software upgrades for after the reproductive years! "

[**Source:** http://www.master-your-dating-tips.com/modern-women-want.html]

Loyalty and Trust

Loyalty and trust are the two most important traits in a partner. Does the partner remain loyal in word and deed? Does the partner defend you to friends and family? What are the whispers about the partner that could indicate breaches of loyalty and trust? What are loyalty and trust indicators?

Although I put loyalty and trust together, there are some differences in the two. The basic difference is loyalty is given because of trust. The congruence of the two is that one must trust the other person in order to contribute loyalty.

There are a lot of sayings about broken trust such as once it is broken it is difficult to rebuild. Difficult, but not impossible. That is a key. The usual problem with trust is that we each have a perception of what the other is doing and should be doing. Doubt creeps into the cracks in what is believed and what seems to be the evidence. How far can one trust another person? Can you trust them with their friends in your absence? Can you trust them with relative strangers in your absence? Can you trust them in any situation to put your relationship and love above all else? How does one build trust?

The first thing about trust is that it is given unconditionally, until events prove otherwise. By events I mean actual proof that the other person did something that affects the relationship.

From my own experiences I can tell you that when my fiancée was reported to have gone out with another boy, I was angry, jealous, and came close to breaking off the engagement. Since we had been apart for a while, me in college and she a high school senior, there was a natural vulnerability to seek company. When we finally got back together after six months, I asked what she did, suspecting the worst. She replied, "I admit going out, but I wanted some company. He knew you from high school and we went out for a coke. Nothing else happened."

Now it was up to me to lay down the law and tell her it was never to happen again or I would take back the ring and break the engagement. We had another eight months to go to the planned wedding date. I knew her mother would tell me if she went out with someone else. The town was very small and word always got back to the parents. Her mother in fact told me she was disappointed that her daughter went out with someone else in the first place and wanted to "strangle her daughter." Parents become emotionally invested in relationships as well and often they can feel the problems in a relationship more than those directly involved .

Here is my consultation for each person to do their own evaluation:

1. Situation Evaluation:

What situations does the other person get into of their own volition? Where do they go for entertainment when you are not available? What kind of establishment do they go into without you being present, let alone that being together you would not even go into some of those establishments?

2. Actions Evaluation:

How does the other person act both in your presence and out of your sight? If they are flirty when you are present, how much more do they flirt when you are not there? What have you heard from friends about them and how they act? A friend may give you a clue without wanting to reveal more, such as "Are you sure you can trust him/her?" Pick up on the little clues. What do they put on their Facebook pages and how do they respond to posts from others?

3. Confirm the Doubts or Validate the Truth:

Don't take one person, or even one friend's story. Doubt does not mean distrust. What it means is that you are deciding on the trust issue each time there is a doubt. If multiple reports come to you, then it is time to discuss the issue or issues with the other person. They may not even be aware that they are doing something to give you doubts and erode your trust.

Do not automatically distrust. We used to have a saying in the On-Site Inspection Agency, "Trust, but verify." That is the right attitude. Continue to trust and sweep away the doubts with communication with the other person in the relationship, or discover the truth and decide whether to end the relationship, but first make an effort to save the relationship by promises together, sharing what went on and rebuilding the trust.

A picture of someone with only the opposite sex around arouses suspicions and unnecessarily opens the relationship up to examination by the person seeing the photo.

Trust like loyalty is not something to be earned, in my opinion. It is something to be given and protected by doing the right things, being with the right crowd, and going to the right places. Going to church is more trustworthy place than a night club or bar.

Age plays a role in trust. A teenager acts often on hormones, not thinking about others or the consequences of actions. The more mature a person becomes the more steps must be taken by both parties to ensure the trust of another in them. Actions speak louder than words, especially in continuing to put the brick and mortar of trust in place.

Loyalty is an act of fealty. Even when trust may be eroding, being loyal to the other person may bring them back and be the foundation for strengthened trust. Loyalty is given even in the face of uncertainty.

The reason for my divorce was one sided loyalty. I gave complete loyalty, but my spouse did not.

Another story. When I was the first U.S. Department of Commerce Foreign Commercial Officer in Vladivostok, Russia, I was separated from my wife. Just prior to departure in July 1993, I told her that I would remain loyal to her and the family and we would be together in a year. I told her I expected her to be loyal to me going to Russia where we had been assigned together in the 1980's. I said, "Do not believe anything the KGB tries to pull such as a picture of me with a woman or some other stupid thing. They can make up composite photographs as they had done many times in the past to trick people and blackmail them." I realized that upon departure for my assignment, my spouse thought I was actually telling her that if I was found in a compromising position, I may actually be guilty."

Four or five months into the assignment I got a call from wife who accused me of having an affair with a Russian woman and asked if I wanted a divorce! "What are you talking about, I asked?" She said, "I received a photo from a government woman there that I had met prior to her going with her husband on assignment. You are sitting at the table with a Russian woman." I was at a loss until I remembered I had invited my Russian language teacher and her mother to the Vlad Motor Inn as a favor. That was all. Where is the trust? Where is the loyalty? After a long pause and her description of the girl I realized someone had taken a picture of me without my knowledge and sent it to my wife.

After a long pause, I said, "Divorce." It was a snap decision, but the disloyalty ran so deep and cut so hard I decided to end our almost thirty year marriage. But, you say, what about communicating together and working it out. We did that three months later, but I ended it. What was the loyalty issue, you may ask?

Asking me about having an intimate relationship over the phone to Russia placed my career in jeopardy because both the Russians and the Americans listened to international telephone calls. I would have a notation in my security file. Furthermore discussing it in depth would not solve the problem. If I had received a letter through diplomatic mail, I could have dealt with it. My wife should have known better than to ask if I wanted a divorce. I had never contemplated it and had never done anything to deserve the question. Her lack of trust and disloyalty especially having told her prior to departure that situations could arise strengthened my resolve to end the relationship. Jealousy is probably the right word for what she felt, but it was the destruction kind.

Upkeep: Cleanliness is Next to Godliness

General personal hygiene and upkeep through the dating process is important for both men and women. Smelling good is an imperative in the modern world. Men often have a problem with this because they work in a less sanitary environment normally. The other problem is they have difficulty distinguishing good cologne from bad and just splash on cheap after shave.

Clean Test: Clean men have a much better chance for acceptance of a date by a female and continuing to be clean throughout the entire relationship shows attention to detail and to the sensitivities of the female. Clean includes no gas emissions. Elsewhere this is shown as a no-no.

Health Test: Body health and body conditioning are essential not only in the attraction process, but in the dating process. Women are look for good genes and general health and ability to keep in shape are indicators the children will be healthy as well.

Smell Test: Good shaving lotion and cologne used by a man are highly important because women use their nose a great more than men in associating with someone. A healthy good smelling body enters the subconscious of the woman and acts as a turn-on. Returning smelly from work is not a problem, but showing up on the first date without smelling good can make a woman leave immediately, in not sooner.

Drugs, Alcohol, and Tobacco: What is worse than a man spitting tobacco into a jar or on the street as a turn off for women? Probably smoking cigarettes and the smell they leave on the breath and on the clothing. Drugs are a powerful indicator that either partner will not be reliable, dependable, or even healthy for very long. Alcohol if consumed moderately by both parties may not be much of a problem, but getting drunk and trying to get the other person drunk are.

Jealousy

This is a good time to bring up jealousy. Jealousy can be protective, but it can also be destructive. I just told you about the destructive kind and will shortly revisit the topic.

Jealousy is a natural human instinct. Jealousy is good and natural in a relationship and there should always be a twinge of wanting to protect the other from all comers. Jealousy is even endearing and helps form a stronger bond of mutual protection. A person who is not jealous does not care, but then I never met someone that was not jealous of someone. I am not referring to the envy kind of jealousy. I am referring to the jealousy of a target person with whom you have made an emotional commitment mentally, whether or not you have told that person of the depth of your commitment and desire to "take them off the market" and build a picket fence around them.

Real Life Scenario #1: What are you doing?

Consider the thought processes at a party. You are at a party with the guy you have been dating for some time. The length of time dating is irrelevant. It can even happen after engagement. A beautiful girl comes over and begins to flirt with your boyfriend even though you are arm in arm. His attention is shifted from you and he is actually smiling at the intruder. The intruder compliments him saying, "I just had to come over and talk to such a handsome boy." Daggers shoot from your eyes, first toward her and then toward him. He is responding to her advances and even compliments her on her appearance. You tug lightly on his arm to pull him away, but he doesn't take the hint, probably because he is oblivious to you, maybe even anesthetized, oh good grief hypnotized. You pull your arm away as another nonverbal signal of disapproval that something is wrong here, but he doesn't seem to notice. Now he raises his hand making silly little gestures using the freed arm.

Sound familiar? It happens thousands of time daily or better put, nightly. What is he doing? How could his attention shift from you? And now it has been thirty minutes and they are still talking and she is still flirting! He is eating it up! You thought you had experienced jealousy before, but nothing compared to the green lasers shooting from your eyes. Jealousy triggers tenuous responses that in psychiatry are known as fight or flight. Are you ready to fight for him? Be the competitive best you can be? Are you ready to run away in tears to the bathroom?

There is an evaluation process that takes all of 30 seconds. What does he see in her? What am I, chopped liver? How can I outdo her? Mentally you start inventorying: hair color, hair style, eye color, skin, height, build, dress or lack of it, makeup, shoes, accent, speech patterns, what she is saying.

The competitive side is capable of anything from saying we have to go to throwing a punch at either party talking. The flight response is actually another mechanism designed to draw away your boyfriend and restore his attention to you.

By the time you reach the car you are beyond green with jealousy. Pupils have dilated to black orbs consuming the entire eyeball. Now what?

Real Life Scenario #2: Where are you?

The technology of communication is fascinating. We can call, text, or message instantly to ask, "Where are you?" We can even track the other person with a GPS device built into the phone so we know how far away the other person is and can make assumptions about what they are doing this time. One little breakdown in this communication link and now the doubts again enter the mind. To make matters worse, every morning for months, he has called you or you have called him to wish a good day for each other. Why did he not call me? Why is he not answering his phone? It has been an hour with no response. Is he dead? Where is he? Who is he with? His cell phone broke and he had to go to work, but you don't know that. You send a message, "Pick up your stupid phone." Your mind is racing and your heartbeat is elevated. Was he with someone last night that made him forget to phone you? No response all day. He is working hard all day. By the end of the day jealousy has consumed you, but you don't know how to direct the hurt and anger.

The potential threat (as far as you know it is just a potential threat), is driving you crazy. What is beyond mad, madness? You feel queasy in the stomach, the heart rate speeds up, you are enraged without a target. He calls you at 8:00 in the evening. Now what?

Real Life Scenario #3: Past Relationships Unexplained

You are on a date and your girlfriend suddenly starts talking about a past flame, or person dated, or you don't know what happened between them. Maybe nothing, maybe the worst you can imagine. Since this is you, your imagination runs to the worst thing. Something triggered her memory banks. Was it the restaurant you just passed, the movie theater over there, the shopping mall to which you are headed? Doesn't matter what triggered her thoughts coming out. What matters is she is sounding sentimental. The past friend was the jerk who left her for another girl and she is talking like this? What actually happened between them? Of course, in this situation everyone will experience at least the pangs of jealousy.

You start comparing yourself to him. All the thoughts the girl had in Scenario 1 come to mind. You start checking available resources. How far do you go and how intrusive do you become. Do you check her purse when she is not looking for pictures or notes? Do you get a transcription of her phone conversations from the phone company? Do you have her followed by a private investigator? Here's an easy one. Check on MySpace or Facebook for any communication between the two. What do they say and what does it mean? How recent was the last communication? What was the tone? The more jealousy that mounts the more you want to interrogate your girlfriend. Now what?

Real Life Scenario #4: Who are you with?

Boys and girls, men and women all have separate friends and groups that they "hang out with" at least on occasion. Boys do go out with pals and girls like to get together with other girls. That is natural to want to be out with friends and talk about things that the other group likes and that are not good conversation starters for either one.

Guys like to talk about and watch sports, compete on computer games, talk about work and jobs, and go fishing or hunting. Some girls may want to do those things, but most would prefer to go out to the mall shopping, go to a nice restaurant, take in a "chick flick," or do other things unfathomable to a guy.

In a group situation leadership principles need to be applied so the group does the right things and a person does not allow themselves to be placed in compromising situations that lead to jealousy. A leader will try to take their friends to the right places and do good things, but if the group turns on them, a leader walks away and says I am not a part of this. Judgment may be exhibited by some at an early age, but it often takes a measure of maturity to play a leadership role and be willing to leave the party when drinking or other inappropriate activities start.

Destructive jealousy is pushing the envelope of protection too far and potentially smothering the relationship. There is a difference prior to engagement and after engagement. Prior to engagement and especially with young people dating each other there are times when they will be apart by school, work, and sports activities.

Psychiatrists make a distinction between attachment and love. Now there's an interesting dichotomy. Attachment is an inward orientation on self and builds self pity by not being with the other person. Attachment comes with entitlement and ownership rights that accrue from a relationship and build in the mind controlling actions and unleashing what is often called the green-eyed monster. The other green-eyed monster being envy. Love is transcendental. Love soars above the fray and is unconditionally given.

Jealousy subsides once we truly love the other person. That is where trust and loyalty come into play. Trust comes from love. Distrust is a constant heartache and result of attachment not being converted to love. In fact the problem you have with jealousy is not with your partner, and heaven forbid it cannot be your fault, but it must be the fault of God who forgot to give you a plan and roadmap on how to get to the end. How could God even consider taking away the one you selected, the one you freely chose, even though you did not take God into the equation in the first place?

The pinpricks or pangs of jealousy will always be there as a defense mechanism, but when two people fall in love, they are under control. Love is unconditional.

A variant of jealousy is between children and parents. A son is often jealous of his father giving attention to the son's girlfriend and finds it difficult when the father calls her beautiful. A daughter is often jealous of her own mother who says you look great tonight to the boyfriend. These are healthy little jealousies that are easily worked out once the age difference is realized and once the son or daughter understands the father or mother are not chasing their date or partner. What did you expect them to say, they are ugly? In fact they are helping to validate your choice. I worry about the mother or father that does not express approval to and for the date. Silence would certainly communicate disapproval or potential disapproval and cause more embarrassment.

Fathers and mothers are jealous too, but on behalf of their son or daughter. They now have a vested interest in the partner and an emotional attachment. Their jealousy is directed to make sure that the other person is in the right places and doing the right things. They relax when they are together, but in social situations pay attention to how the other person is treated and acts when in the company of other sons or daughters.

Forgiveness

The Bible says to forgive as our Father in heaven forgives us. (Colossians 3:13) Even when trust may be broken it can be repaired through forgiveness and empathy. Another saying is forgiveness is next to godliness. But what can be forgiven? Certainly things that occurred when neither party thought they were in a relationship are easier to forgive than those things that occur when a person is inside a relationship. To answer the question, everything can be forgiven if one wants to do so.

Forgiveness cannot be a constant thing where one begins to compromise themselves by forgiving the other over and over. There is a cutoff point to the relationship, especially prior to marriage. Communication with God, praying together, separating themselves by boundaries from others will improve the chances of trust being regained. Forgiveness has to be unconditional, because you are forgiving the other for everything. You are forgiving all the past transgressions against your sensitivities both of omission and commission.

Forgiveness is not easy. We do not come by it naturally. Our natural instincts are to retreat into protecting the self and punishing the offender. We feel anger toward the other person and betrayal.

The first response is to strike out at the other person and get them back for what they did, or as often is the case, what we think they did.

The right response is to take it to the Lord in prayer. Ask for God to heal the wound(s), restore or break the relationship as is his will and plan for your life, and see what happens. God bears the scars. God knows the plan. God knows what will happen. The Gospel Mark has a good perspective: *And when you stand praying, if you hold anything against anyone, forgive him, so that your Father in heaven may forgive you your sins. (NIV) Mark 11:25*

Now there is a perspective. Have we done something ourselves to cause the other person to do something we do like. God is the judge.

There are several passages in the Bible regarding forgiveness including not judging others, forgiving seventy times seven, forgive that you will be forgiven. We forgive by obedience to God's will, place the matter before the Lord and letting him deal with the offender, and have faith. The feelings of forgiveness may take some time. Time is also useful for gauging the remorse of the other person.

Acceptance of apologies and explanations for actions as well as promises that things will not happen again that are against our sensitivities is part of the process. There may have been circumstances beyond the control of the other person. What about a surprise bachelor party given by supposed friends and they hired strippers to perform? That is a circumstance that takes some understanding and immediate forgiveness because the wedding is next in a day or two.

How do we know we have forgiven? The heart is actually relieved, tension and stress are gone, we are ready to move on to either a better relationship or finding another one even though we have forgiven the other. The one who suffers the most grief, anger, resentment, and bitterness is the one who cannot forgive. Forgiveness then is therapeutic, a feeling of peace and freedom. That freedom is then available to resurrect the relationship or with experience and eyes wide open move toward a more perfect one. Claim the reward of forgiveness.

Keeping Secrets

The ability to keep secrets between a dating couple, engaged couple, and later married couple builds trust and shows loyalty. In the modern era of the 21st Century with communications all around us, keeping secrets is more difficult, but never more important.

Refer to the love poem in Chapter 11. Love does not boast and is not puffed up. Boasting is more than disclosing secrets; it is puffing and adding untruths. Boasting about sexual exploits is common among both men and women. I warn everyone to keep what is in your relationship secret between only the two of you.

Look Ahead to Marriage

No one should date a person unless they have an initial impression that they might make a future husband or wife. Often the first attraction is physical and young people do not consider the rest of the equation. Dating, going steady, engagement period are all times for evaluation. When it comes to engagement, final preparations should be underway and planning for a wedding date is the target for completing all the things that can be done in preparation for marriage and the marriage night.

Chapter 4

"Let's Get Together, Yay, Yay, Yay!"

PARDON ME FOR A reference to an old Rock and Roll song, but it seemed so appropriate. "Let's get together, yay, yay, yay!" Excitement time. Excitement not just for the boy and girl, but for their families. Something new occurred. A change in relationships possibly will arise.

The Dating Game: High Risks, High Rewards

Dating is more than a game. It is high stakes poker with high risks and high rewards as well as potentially devastating losses when you go "all in." Let's discuss the dating game at the very beginning before the first date. What is important to each person on the date? How do we act? What manners are exhibited? There are some principles I have developed over years of personal experience and observation.

Principle #1: Never Bring a Friend Along on A Date Unless There is A Double Date

Circumstances may dictate a double date such as not having a car, going to a first party, insistence of the other person on a safe dating experience, or a blind date introduction. Those are understandable circumstances and must be presented in advance to the date as the only alternatives for the first time out. Other than that, the first principle of dating is NEVER EVER include a friend. Elvis Presley had a great song that applies to dating and friends being involved:

That's When Your Heartaches Begin

Love is a thing you never can share
And when you bring a friend into your love affair,
That's the end of your sweetheart
That's the end of your best friend
That's when the heartaches begin.

What possible motivations are there for bringing along a friend? Excuses range from soothing nerves on a first date; impressing a boy or girl with a friend that is judged to have more experience, charm, and status; learning how to behave properly; looking less eager for a kiss; or prepping the friend to provide compliments about you and your prowess in some field or area. Only the emotionally insecure bring along a friend. The amazing fact is the emotionally insecure are in the majority.

The view of the person you are dating is they see a lack of leadership, insecurity (which is the truth), and lack of trust (fear of what might happen). Lack of leadership means that everything done requires a poll and must be approved by everyone on the date. Insecurity means mistrust of one's judgment or fear of messing up demonstrating a lack of self confidence. If there is a lack of trust, why go on the date in the first place? Girls want to date someone who demonstrates leadership, shows respect, has good manners, and is self confident. They don't want a "wuss".

This does not mean that going to a birthday party with another couple or doing things together with others are out. What it does mean that for early dating and building relationships the couple must be alone without interference to determine for themselves the suitability of the other.

Principle #2: The guy pays unless...

The person doing the inviting pays unless the boy/man offers or even better takes the bill when it comes to the table or pays for the movie tickets. A guy can never go wrong by picking up the tab even when invited. Exceptions to this rule are of course, someone else has already paid, the girl/woman received free tickets, or the girl works at Disneyland and has free passes for the summer. In western society in particular, however, the boy or man pays for the restaurant tab and the tickets for events.

Principle #3: Arrive on Time

Always arrive on the minute or earlier, not later. I have a story to share about the first date of my mother and father that shows early arrival to the extreme. My father (not yet) lived 60 miles away from the town in which my mother lived. They had met at a Christian rally and decided to go on a first date at 6 pm on the next Saturday night. The morning of the date came and my mother's grandma with whom she was living at the time, went to the window around 6 o'clock in the morning and exclaimed, "Minette, get up! There is someone in a car out front." My mother came to the window and began laughing uncontrollably. "That is my date for tonight and he is twelve hours early." "Well, invite him in to spend the day." My great grandmother was extremely pleased to have time to spend with her grandchild's first date and my mother was blown away by the concern for reaching her in time over the roads that were dirt in the late 1930's. Perhaps it is never too early to arrive, however, I recommend five minutes early just in case.

Principle #4: Leave your emotional bags at home

The first date is not a therapy session. Besides you do not want to divulge problems for the other to deal with on the first date. The psycho-sicko boss, teacher, or parent is not something to place on the other's doorstep, at least not yet. The cheating ex is not someone to bring into the conversation. This is an exploratory date. If the other party brings something like that up be sensitive, but take control and steer the conversation another direction.

On subsequent dates minor disclosures are fine. Open one little carrying case at a time and do not dwell on it. Of course respond in a positive manner if the date wants to know, because that shows the date is concerned about you and there is nothing to worry about. Do not unpack the entire case.

Principle # 5: Focus on the other person

Pay a lot of attention to the other person. If you are in a crowd, don't come down with roving eye syndrome assessing other possibilities. Ask innocuous questions about the interests, goals, dreams, and realities of the other person. This is not a time to probe and not a time to give an intelligence quiz. Don't ask, "What does your mother think of us dating?" Believe me the other person normally doesn't have a clue yet what their parents think. You really don't care and don't want to know the answer to that question anyway. It is irrelevant to your relationship at least for now. Similarly you don't need a *Wunderlich* test question given to professional athletes such as, "If you were an animal, which one would you be?" You want to make each other comfortable, not give a pass/fail question.

Principle #6: Stay on safe topics

The weather might be the safest, but it is boring. Events at school, sports, world events, television shows, movies, and personal interests are safe (usually) and ice breakers. Stay with topics that seem of interest to the other person. The date will not feel threatened and they will love to share. For them the time will pass quickly and they will feel they had a wonderful date regardless of whether it is sitting at a car at a fast food restaurant, or in a sophisticated place.

Principle #7: Show a sense of humor. Laugh and smile

Most of us are attracted to fun witty dates who demonstrate a sense of humor and ability to laugh at what happens. Don't do it on purpose as a test, but if a coke falls in the other person's lap or your own, laugh a little and get them to see the humor. Smiling is the surest way to another person's subconscious. If something happens to you, show a good sense of humor, laugh at yourself at least a little, make a witty comment about your predicament, or repeat something funny with a smile and laugh. It may be more funny the second time.

Principle #8: Prepared Spontaneity

Opportunities for romantic interludes may present themselves without preparation and they are often the best chances for a more intimate encounter of the best kind. If the restaurant is near a beach or lake, suggest taking a stroll along the beach or lakeside. I call this a mood enhancer. Relationship experts generally agree that the number one way to generate interest in you is to bring some excitement to the date that is appropriate. A walk in the park, a ride around an interesting area nearby, or a visit to an amusement park, are all things that can seem spontaneous, even though you have thought them out.

On later dates, more provocative things can be done such as taking a date to a scary movie, a scary boat ride, or scary fast motorbike ride. Endomorphins are produced in the brain that while stimulating fear in the mind, also create sexual desire.

Principle #9: Appropriate physical signals

Neuro-linguistic specialists observe body language and know the power of understanding how a person feels from the way they stand, sit, or look. Crossing arms, for example, means back off, I am closed to what you are saying. Some ways to communicate with body language that subtly influences the other person are to stand facing the other person, look into the eyes of the date, smile, laugh at whatever seems laughable, lean over toward them a little when talking. Do not lean too far forward or the signal may be misunderstood. Use it subtly during a conversation to influence the other.

A good approach learned from sales classes is mirror the gestures of the other and then take control by moving your hands. The mimicking process makes the other person feel comfortable and as though you really understand them. Then you can control their body language without them realizing what they are projecting.

A touch can be electric and reassuring at the same time. Holding a hand, or patting a partner on the shoulder or back is encouraging and a friendly gesture that the date is being enjoyed. Women love it when a man places his hand on the small of her back. She feels protected, guided, led, and secure.

Principle #10: Complete the date on a high note

Bad date? Complete the date on a high note, unless you are running from danger. By high note, I mean upbeat compliments such as thank you for taking me out. This phrase does not say much and is safe, regardless of the date and circumstances. Completing the date does not mean you are planning on accepting another one with the creep. Lack of a kiss may mean there is no future in this relationship, although it may also mean shyness, inexperience, or lack of one's own confidence. Be content in knowing that you have made a friendship a little stronger.

Good date? Say you had a great time and would like to go again on a date. There is nothing wrong with this coming from either the boy or girl or both. Affirmation is a prelude to a second date and ends the evening on a high note. A kiss is perhaps the best note to end the evening and shows both want more in the future. Later I mention how to kiss, but the idea is not to kiss too long or too passionately. You don't want to appear too eager or too easy to get. Keep the mystery going a little longer.

First Date and Don't Be Late

The first date is a collection mission, but probably for most it is just being with another person for the first time and feeling wanted by someone they like. I am not going to suggest an age to start dating. Ages are culturally derived, not an absolute. In many countries of the world marriages are arranged and often at the age of puberty or around 12 years of age. In the Bible by the age of 12 girls were already betrothed.

In America dating is usually around the time one person or the other gets their driver's license. When I got married, I was 21 and my wife was 17 and we had dated one year and been engaged for another. My wife had to get a signed permission by her mother at the Court House to get married. I still remember the application process and her mother waiting to sign. Yes. That means she was 15 when we started dating and I was 19.

Not only do the two people dating collect intelligence on each other, the parents begin their research, oh they don't call it that, on the person their son or daughter is dating. What do they already know from sports, social gatherings, friendships with the other family, church groups, on the street? What do they need to know? Panic sets in. Who is this person wanting to be with their son or daughter? What are their intentions? Why did they choose this one?

As a former intelligence officer, I suppose I can give a list of items particularly for parents, let's call them dating collection requirements.

Dating Collection Requirements

1. Name. Obviously this is the first requirement. Do you already know this person?

2. Address: What is the proximity? What is the neighborhood?

3. Phone Number and other means of communications such as email, <u>Facebook MySpace</u>, and texting.

4. Church affiliation: Do they go to the same church? Do they go to a compatible church? Catholics versus Protestants plus Baptists is often a problem.

4. Friends: Who do you know that knows him or her? What is their reputation? Who they hang out with to use the modern vernacular is important.

5. Age: Is there a major difference in age?

6. Race: Is there a problem with a son or daughter dating a person of a different race?

7. Education: What education do they have? What education do they seek?

8. Activities: Do they play sports? Do they play in the school band? Do they play musical instruments? What are their hobbies? This last one is particularly useful for planning on giving a Christmas gift or birthday present.

9. Parents: Do you know the parents? Do they come from a single family home or a foster care system? This question helps with sensitivities and is nothing against the other person.

10. Employment: If out of school, are they employed? For whom do they work? Is this a temporary job, or a career move? Are they employed while in school? What do they do with their money? Save? Buy a car or truck?

11. Affiliations: Political? Social? Networking? Fringe Groups? Danger Groups? What do you mean danger groups, you ask? Is there a potential for violence or activism that could get them in trouble and your son or daughter along with them? I classify a coven or witchcraft group as a threat to the son or daughter and to the family as well. That is but one example. Investigate the groups. An innocent sounding name may hide an evil purpose or may harbor criminal intent.

12. Brothers and Sisters: Do they have brothers or sisters? What do we need to know about them?

These twelve questions are a good start to the list. Everyone should continue with their own list. Most parents simply do not have a plan in mind and just get whatever information falls in their lap. An active collection agenda is good for everyone.

Don't interrogate on the first date, but do think about filling out the list at least mentally if not in your diary. Return to the Principles of Dating above for what to do on the first date. In addition to the ten principles of dating give flowers on the first date. That starts the mood right and impresses the parents of your thoughtfulness.

Assume the first date was successful, now what? Should I call, or should I wait?

Aftermath of Round 1. Does it Add Up?

I will assume that you had a good first date and get out of bed the next morning thinking about how good it was to be dating and how nice the evening went and concluded. Who makes the next move? It may depend on whether there is a natural meeting place such as the halls of school, or the classroom at college. These are natural meeting places and make it easy to engage in conversation even if slightly coded to avoid others knowing how things went. Assuming that is not the case, who moves first to establish contact? One of you has to take the initiative. Consider the other person. If they are shy in conversation, but worth it, the more extroverted person should do the contacting.

The traditional answer of course was the boy had to call first, but tradition often said let it bake for a day or two. Women were taught that to avoid appearing to "chase" a man, they had to wait. Fear of rejection by either party after a good date is a problem as well. Women are usually apprehensive about calling first. Society has made them that way. It is not just the tradition, but consider the phone being picked up and a female voicing answering. Did I just date a married man? Is this his mother? You want to talk to him, not to whatever "her" answered. There is nothing wrong with the woman making contact first, but it works best with sensitive or shy men. Whoever calls first is taking an initiative and responsibility for the course of the relationship.

When not to call: Do not call first out of frustration to ask, 'Why haven't you called me?" Bad move. Instruction in the common laws of decency is not high on the priority list of the other person.

Relationship experts advise not to call the next morning after a first date or even the first few subsequent dates. The most time, however, to wait is three days before taking the initiative. This establishes an early formality to the relationship that is not overly aggressive or overly rude. Waiting a little is what I call a percolation technique that allows replays of the first date in the mind and develops a stronger feeling to want to simply hear the voice of the other person.

Women should understand that the dated person is not running around with other women unless that is his reputation. More than likely he is sitting at home watching the football game, eating a delivered pizza, and thinking about you.

Regardless of who makes the first call, timing is the key and tact is crucial. Unless you meet regularly at some location such as school or work where there is an automatic opportunity daily to communicate, I suggest early evening between 7 and 8 pm as the most ideal time. Don't call a place of work. The office policy may well dictate no personal calls, and believe me the mood is not right. Responses are controlled with coworkers hovering nearby.

Sending flowers or gifts is not a good idea either unless you are extremely serious. You are not stalking the other person, just looking for a response and hoping for another date.

The phone rings. The heart quickens. Could it be him/her? It is! Now what? Make an effort to control surprise, joy, ecstasy and modulate the voice with a mild touch of enthusiasm. It is probably not a good idea to say, "I have been waiting by the phone three days for your call!" It is probably not a good idea either to blurt out, "You are my Prince Charming." The idea of another date and being together is still in the conceptual stage and there is no commitment that should be made by either one.

The phone doesn't ring. Now what? You may not have been rejected, but may not have been a priority yet. The person who took you on a date may be temporarily constrained by parents or out of money. All is not lost. Don't get mad, but do call in an even voice. Express your candid opinion of the first date and recall some interesting or even exciting moments if there were any. Let the conversation take its course, whether an excuse from the other for not calling, or a statement by the other that he/she did not call because they thought you would not like it.

Surprising to say, some people live in fear of rejection by you, not just you fearing their rejection. The call gives the chance for both to change the course of the future. Understand that the first date is really just an experiment anyway to see if there is even common grounds for a relationship. You are not yet in a relationship, you are in limbo.

Some writers recommend not calling the other person, if there is no call say after five days. I disagree. You need to find out the truth. You have a right to know if there is any hope for a future relationship. Do not assume rejection, but listen to the clues by the other person during the conversation.

I say better to be certain and put the date behind you if a rejection than to wonder forever. There is no need to ask why or why not? Just assume that if there is no second date, there are more opportunities. Don't change yourself just to accommodate one person's opinion.

Second Date and Subsequent Dates

A second date is like a second helping of food. It means there was something to the first date and interest is piqued in how a second date will turn out. Fun is not the object, sharing is. A second date is a validation for both that things went well on the first date and so far I have not discovered anything to warn me away. A man usually has made a decision already about a second date in the first few minutes after ordering food at a restaurant, or after drinks are served.

A second date is still a get acquainted process. Do they like the same places you do? Did they ask where you would like to go? This is particularly important for the girls. If not on the second date, then by the fifth date, have they taken your request into account? Will they come to church with you?

A second date is an opportunity to make a different impression or reinforce positively the first impression. A second date should be a relief and a time to open up a little more and communicate in a more comfortable atmosphere. You can either keep the second date simple, as is the case with younger dating couples, or more imaginative as is necessary for more advanced couples to enhance interest and improve chances for romance.

Guidance on the second date is as important as guidance on the first date. Don't forget the flowers. Flowers are safest. Save the box of chocolates until you are assured your date is not on a diet. Do not bring the bottle of wine until you find out if she even drinks alcohol. Jewelry, articles of clothing, and perfume are more intimate and should not be given until an ongoing relationship has been formed. I have condensed some ideas that are based on extensive research.

Idea #1: Up the ante

The first date was to get acquainted and so a place, such as a restaurant provided a place to talk and get to know more about each other. Now it is time to up the ante, but do it carefully. If the idea is a movie, it must be chosen wisely to avoid offense by indiscrete language or sexually oriented content. A dramatic theme is more appreciated than an action move and increases the romantic mood. Action thrillers can be a downer for the girl.

Idea #2: Change the venue

The first date place is often special. Save it for another time and return to it such as on the one month anniversary of dating. You have a chance to find out more from another setting or activity. How about an amusement park complete with rides and candy apples? Find a place such as this to laugh and play a little bit while increasing physical contact such as holding hands, a gesture that brings security and comfort to both daters. I could give a range of places, but each location is unique and the concept here is to make a plan.

Idea #3: Tell the other person where you are going and what you are doing

Did you forget to tell her you were going horseback riding? She appears in a designer miniskirt. I am imagining the discussion at the stables and am still laughing. If the boy/man does not tell where you are going in advance, the girl/woman should always ask anyway. Parents need to know their daughter is going to a safe place and what kind of place they can be found in an emergency. The girl/woman needs to know how to dress appropriately for the occasion.

Idea #4: Compliments and jokes are a good thing

Not all jokes are funny, but a little titter is appreciated even for a bad joke. Do not tell an off color joke or one with a sick punch line. Flattery works. The old saying is "Flattery will get you everywhere." Let me give you a little warning about flattery. If flattery is insincere or excessive, you will be discovered to be a fraud.

Compliments bestowed on the date partner are endearing and confidence building. Never criticize on the second date even slightly unless the partner has done something so outrageous it is time to go home and forget about them. Saying in a public restaurant, I see your tan is fading will not endear you to the other person.

Idea #5: Either Date can physically touch. Don't be afraid.

Touching appropriately is OK on the second date. Gestures of physical affection such as placing an arm around you, playing with your hair, or holding you close while kissing are fine. Be receptive and respond in kind. The male should make the first move, but some men have heard stories about the touchiness of women and are actually afraid to initiate physical contact. Women in contemporary America can initiate physical intimate contact as well.

Idea #6: Dress smartly

If there are a range of places, dress comfortably, but smartly. Avoid high heels until you know you are going to church or the opera. Appropriate dress means both comfort with the surroundings and confidence in appearance. Dressing smartly does not mean go buy some new dresses. It means wear something that fits properly and looks good on you whether it came from WalMart or Target.

Idea #7: Flirting is a good thing, but only with the date

Trust me on this one! Do not flirt with anyone, but the person that brought you. Men or women sometimes flirt on the side in a vain attempt to make themselves look popular with the opposite sex, but the date partner will interpret it as an insult. Besides, you look foolish flirting on a date with the other people with whom you are flirting. You are not searching every minute for more possibilities. You are trying to pin down the present shot you have.

Flirting with the date is a way of communicating you are fun and have a sense of humor as do I. You are improving your chances of a sustained relationship by flirting. Flirting says, "I am interested in you and I can be exciting." Flirting is a way of complimenting the other in a fun way. Flirting impresses us, is attention that is gratuitous, and is safe. Returning the flirt is confirmation and validation the other person is doing something right and gives them confidence.

Idea #8: Laugh off disagreements unless they are overwhelming

Disagreement is natural unless one wants to become a sycophant. A sycophant is not a sick elephant. A sycophant is someone who cannot bear disagreement and always subordinates their thoughts and ideas to another. On the second date you are not yet engaged in a power play. No, you are not! Laugh off disagreement. Find the humor in yourself and in the other person. If agreement is not on the way, agree to disagree.

Idea #9: It is too early to commit

The dating experience, especially the first few dates is way too early to make promises to each other. The best policy is don't ask, don't tell! Commitment comes much farther down the road. There are too many questions, too many possibilities including other dates, too many pitfalls to overcome at this stage. That does not mean that an early commitment is doomed to failure. I do believe in love at first sight.

Idea #10: Sex is out of the Question on the first or second date

Don't even go there. I doubt you know anything about the other's sexual history and past partners, if any. For mature individuals understood sex may be part of the equation and the reason for the date in the first place. Now we are in conflict with God's plan if we are engaging in sex with every person we date. For those that do plan on sex by date number two, bring appropriate birth control items in purse or pocket.

Even in advanced dating at more mature ages psychologists tell us that six dates should be considered before advancing to having a sexual relationship. One does need to learn something about the sexual history and assess the possibility of life altering and life threatening diseases.

You have now made it through the second date and there is more ahead.

Chapter 5

Romance Rules

WE ARE NOW SOMEWHERE way beyond the second date. We are in a romantic relationship. Now what? The road to the altar is not smoothly paved with rose petals. This chapter suggests making a personal inventory of what makes you happy. The next step is the qualities you want in a relationship and marriage. This chapter then turns to the differences between a Romeo (boy or man) and a Juliet (girl or woman).

Romantic Rules

The last chapter asked, what is love? Now the question is, what is romance and what do I want out of the romance. Let's start with the no-no's, look at ourselves, and then decided on the qualities that are the most pleasing in a romantic relationship.

Never Ever...

Rule #1: You already know Rule #1, No Friends:
Never ever bring a friend into your love affair either as a tag along or as an arbiter in an argument. That ruins everything. Friends are at the very least an impediment, at the worst they want to separate the happy couple. I just said it in the previous chapter and it is worth repeating. Keep friends away except for special occasions like a birthday, or an occasional walk with another couple, but never, and I mean never have

a friend around your girlfriend or boyfriend for an evening or take them places such as a movie. Three is not only a crowd it is dangerous.

Rule #2: If a person drinks, do so only in moderation.

This is obvious -- never get drunk. When you are out of control, your future is out of control. Not only are sexual inhibitions released, but you could end up with the wrong partner for the night and lose the whole romantic relationship you had worked on so hard. Drinking makes fools of everyone.

Rule #3: Never lie.

Wow! That sounds easy until the questions open up the past. The wise person becomes adept as sidestepping direct questions about the past, just as the wise person does not ask in the first place. There are natural times for a few details from the past to come out. Some come out regardless of our intentions to keep them hidden. An ex-boyfriend or girlfriend meets you at a party and begins to regale the entire crowd on your past sexual exploits and partners. Get them to shut up by all means, but meet the accusations head on after the party with your paramour and tell the truth, at least in bits and pieces. Believe me, they do not want to hear the whole sordid tale, but their curiosity has been aroused and you will need to approach this head on, but with tact and diplomacy..

A little dose of truth is sufficient. Too much honesty is overwhelming and scary. The best strategy in romance is to judiciously sprinkle the truth and then only if asked. This takes us to the fourth rule.

Rule #4: Do not share too much.

I have already indicated that. A romance is not a confessional and your romantic partner is not the priest. You don't get ten "Hail Marys" and absolution. Keep your mystique. Keep some things for the marriage. Over sharing is oversaturation. Too much does damage. If all personal qualities and ideas are exposed, it can turn the other person off.

Rule #5: Never say too much. Watch your tongue.

Talking is not necessarily sharing. Talking can serve as a defense mechanism and assist with Rule #4. I cannot count the number of people that think they are witty and want so much to tell the world including personal details about a romance. Conversation is just like alcohol, never stray beyond moderation. What may be open for discussion for you may be desired to be kept a secret by your lover. Sarcasm is delightful only in small quantities and with a smile or smirk. Continuing sarcasm is taken as criticism of the date and where they have taken you for the evening.

Rule #6: Never, but never say "I love you" without meaning it.

There is a difference in men and women saying I love you, not that the intention is not on the same plane. It is. If said too early in a relationship by the woman, the man afraid of commitment could be gone with the wind. Men are more afraid of being tied down than women. Women are the settlers (sometimes referred to as nesters) with time clock ticking and wanting to be in a committed relationship. This does not mean men are seeking something else. The man's time clock is set differently and maturity comes later than for a woman.

When a man tells a woman he loves her, he is now opening himself up and has committed himself to the relationship with all that entails.

Rule #7: Never beg or appear needy

Begging for something from the other person, especially for sex, is the greatest weakness that can be shown. Appearing not to be in a state of need for affection, or attention, or sex, increases the likelihood of getting all those things.

Rule #8: Never need to say, "I'm sorry."

On the television series, NCIS, Jethro Gibbs has a rule, "Never say you're sorry." In a romantic relationship the idea is never to have to say those words. Saying you are sorry once or twice may actually be an endearing quality, if it is sincere. If there are a lot of those, there is a distinct problem and things are not as they should be. Too many times of saying I'm sorry means goodbye, I can't take it anymore.

Rule #9: Never leave each other angry and never go to bed angry with the other person.

This rule is a big one. This is the same rule you must have heard about a marriage. Some of us internalize anger and get very quiet. Some of us get it quickly out of our system. All of us can harbor a grudge or resentment unspoken and sometimes even unrecognized. At the end of a date, at the end of an evening phone call, at the end of the day when going to bed together, the only policy that makes sense is to get rid of anger through communication. I do not mean shouting and yelling, although this is prevalent in some cultures and some families.

If the partner comes from one of those cultures or families, someone is going to have to adjust their rhetoric downward and it may take soothing, cajoling, or counter yelling to get it done. Then the task is to tell the other person you cannot live with that type of pain and tension. Make sure you never leave the other person in an angry mood.

Rule #10: Fight Fairly.

Here is a tough rule. The rules of fighting are different than fighting someone of your own sex. A disagreement may be a "fight" and neither one realizes it. Boys, Men, you do know by now never to strike a girl/woman. Right? This is another never, ever rule. Conflict can strengthen a relationship whether on a date, being engaged, or being married.

Ground Rules for a Fair "Fight"

Fighting fairly requires setting and understanding of the rules of fighting. There are a lot of self-help guides to setting the rule from a variety of sources. I have condensed them down into the following rules that should be discussed before a disagreement or escalation of the conflict. One way to get over the first "spat" or "argument" is for one of the partners to say, "Let's set some ground rules." Just discussing the ground rules can make each other laugh, or least contain the conflict.

1. Fight to resolve, not to win.

The object is not to win, but to settle with the relationship still intact. Think of it more as a negotiation, than a winner takes all. Believe me, the winner will not take all and the source(s) of conflict will remain unless settled.

2. Fight without violence or verbal abuse.

How many of you have read of the college athlete losing a scholarship, losing a girlfriend, and even going to jail for physical violence? Physical violence from either partner is abuse. Understand when it happens, that the other person may have come from a home life in which violence and physical abuse is the norm. That is one of the reasons to discuss the ground rules or how about this suggestion, have them read this set of rules from the book?

Verbal abuse does not scar the body, but does the soul. Yelling and screaming may let off steam, but it is a sure way to escalate the fight unless the other party has a lot of experience at self control and has a calm personality.

3. Fight on the subject.

Fighting can quickly bring up a host of past transgressions, grievances that have been harbored unresolved, and unhealthy little nagging things that have bothered each person. Agree to dispense with one issue at a time. That does not mean you cannot make a list of the little things. In fact, putting it down on paper is a good way to work through issues of any size. The list then becomes the subject. And another thing…

4. Fight on specifics, not on generalities.

Keeping to the key interrogatories of who, what, when, where, why, and how make the grievance concrete and focuses the argument. Juliet said, "I saw you flirting with Jezebel the other day at the high school quad." Now we are getting specific, rather than saying, "You always flirt with girls, don't you?" Romeo might not have a clue that he flirted with Jezebel. At least it allows Romeo a fair chance to defend himself, rather than trying to figure out how many, where, and how often.

Avoid phrases like: You always…You never…You can't… Using such terms actually helps the case of the other partner, because much like on affirmed act in a legal debate is used to destroy the arguments of the opposition, the same can be said for an argument. It only takes the partner one minute to bring up a case of not being always, and the whole weight of the evidence shifts in his favor. You don't want to give him or her that opening in the argument.

5. Fight without involving third parties.

No friends, no coworkers, no relatives. Oh, particularly no relatives. You don't need their judgment on behalf of one or the other. Friends and peers are going to be biased anyway and since when did they have your interests at heart? The friend may be motivated to break up the couple, either because of jealousy for the relationship or wanting to get with the other person. Never listen to a friend. Go to this book. If married with children, find a place to argue/discuss/negotiate/fight outside their viewing and listening space.

6. Fight without past histories.

I pluralized that because both sides of the conflict have a past history of some kind. For one side to bring it up opens the gates for the other to throw something back. This is rather like opening up a line of questioning in a legal trial only to have the other side come back at you. Remember the old saying, "Pointing a finger at someone means four fingers are pointed back at you."

7. Fight without name calling.

That means even endearing names used in the past for each other, because regardless of the intention the name used will be taken as an insult or sound sarcastic to the other, especially with an elevated voice saying it or emotions conditioning it. Names like liar and stupid should not be used without clear evidence of the lie or the other party having a low IQ. I doubt you have either situation with someone you yourself selected for a relationship. If so, you are the one with those qualities in the first place. You are calling yourself a liar and stupid.

8. Fight without accusing.

One of the first things that comes to mind, if not during the last stage of the argument, is to accuse and blame the other person. Accusations escalate. Blame gets out of control. None of us is blameless in the first place, so why start blaming the other person. Usually the crux of the problem is that the other person believes he or she did something or forgot to do something. The issue does need to be brought up in a way that dampers the blame. How can we do that?

The first subordinate principle or corollary if you will is not to use the words, "You did xxx, or you said xxx." Talk instead about your feelings and how you understood the situation. There is no way you can fathom the depth of feelings in the other person, but you hopefully are an expert on your own feelings. "I feel" is how you still have emotions about what was said or not said, what was done or not done. "I felt" refers to the time of the incident. How you felt is relevant to the argument and communicates how you will feel in the future if the same type of event occurs.

9. Communicate, don't berate.

Remember a fight is actually a negotiation tactic to change something. There are several aspects to communication. Respect your partner, mate, or spouse. Respect changes communication and tactics. Respect means "don't hit below the belt." You want this to be fair and you want a result or solution that is sufficient. Using humor in a fight is not a good tactic unless you have an impeccable sense of timing and can deliver the humor in a non-sarcastic and non-injurious way. Laughing at someone's point could become the next issue and injure the sensitivities of the other person.

Active listening, engaging the eyes of the other person, hearing them out before interjecting are all solid communication skills that most people have to develop over time. Gestures and body language often tell more than the words. Is the other person agitated, are they throwing up their hands, are the finger pointing. From reading this book and putting it into practice I assume you are the calm one and not doing the gesturing or getting your body all worked up to the point of jumping up and down.

Escalating, raising the stakes, becoming emotional show a lack of good communication skills. Crying is like the baby who does not get his way. Crying at the end together, however, lets out emotion in a shared setting and wins the heart of the other for showing the depth of their grief or hurt.

Stay calm. Don't raise your voice! "I am in this small room with you and can hear a whisper."

Silence is not communicating and "silence is not golden," except engendering frustration and creating more anger in both parties. There must be feedback.

Inventions of the mind or exaggeration of the situation weaken your own argument, so why try this tactic in the first place. You are losing the communication battle if you bring these into the conversation. Remain focused on facts. You are more believable and the issue is more likely to be resolved amicably.

How about reaching for the hand of your mate or lightly touching the arm? When done in a non-threatening way, the effects can be amazing. Touching calms the other on down and shows you both care and love them. It puts both of you in proximity and reduces tension.

10. Timing.

Saving little things up in the mind until it explodes as the "last straw" is not fair to either party. Iron out small things while they are still small and perhaps the larger "fights" will never come. In your ground rules you can set a time limit for arguing, such as ten or fifteen minutes on the subject. Having this ground rule in place before any arguments, lays down a number that can be used by either party to call a timeout without seriously offending the other party.

Take a "grief" break. If the partner refuses to discuss the issue at hand, call a timeout, but set an appointment and put it on the calendar for sometime during the next 24 hours. The sooner, the better. If the time has gone by for 48 hours, it must not have been that important in the first place. Let it go.

If you need a timeout during a lengthy "discussion" be sure to communicate that to the other person. The steps recommended by counselors are:

1. Take responsibility for breaking off the conversation. Say something like, "I need a timeout," or "I don't want to lose control."
2. Tell the person with whom you are arguing, I need to take a deep breath. I need a time out. Whether you are going to the bathroom, outside for fresh air, or to the balcony for a few minutes tell your partner what you are doing. "I have to go to the bathroom." I am going outside for fresh air and to think." "I am going for a short walk."
3. Set a time for return, or even invite the partner to go along. The break in the action is good for both and clears the heads of those involved.

Using these simples steps will keep the partner from feeling rejected, abandoned, even angrier. Following these steps still shows your partner you are committed to communication and resolution. Your partner might also think if you can sort out your thought things will go their way. What usually happens is both parties realize their pigheadedness and are ready for accommodation upon the return of the other.

Conflict Management

Study this book. I have given you twenty conflict management techniques. Ten of them are what to do to build a relationship and ten are for fighting fairly.

Put the other first. Your partner, your relationship, your marriage, your love, and your trust are at stake.

Listen. Always be ready to listen.

Ending an Argument or Fight

It takes two to tango and it takes two to fight; therefore, it only takes one to stop. The problem though is the terms on which the fight is stopped. Stopping is not easy, but there are some natural breaks when one party or the other figures things are somewhat in balance and can break off the fight.

Asking forgiveness and being willing to forgive is a better way for saying I am sorry. Do not walk out the door without a kiss. Put everything behind. Just as a good athlete does not dwell on the mistakes of the past, so a couple must put the past behind them and leave it there.

For Christians another way is "Take your burden to the Lord and leave it there." Prayer will lay it at God's feet. He will answer in ways of which we did not dream.

Goal Setting

There are two times to set goals: early in a relationship and later in preparation for marriage. In this chapter we will talk about short, medium, and long term goals for a romantic relationship leading up to engagement and then marriage.

Short Term Goals

Short term goals for the relationship are rather easy to assemble.

1. Good dating experiences

2. Having your tastes and interests accounted for

3. Ensuring you have the right romancer

4. Open communication

5. Sharing

6. Elimination of obstacles

7. Sufficient attention

8. Emotional needs being met

9. Protection from others

10. Security and Confidence in both yourself and your Romeo

Medium goals

1. Satisfying relationship

2. Elimination of the competition

3. Love and respect

4. Adjusting to the other persons tastes and interests

Long range goals

1. Engagement

2. Marriage

Chapter 6

Romeo, Juliet, Brutus and Jezebel

As the best seller book was titled in my time, "Women are from Venus and Men are from Mars." Men may even be from Pluto, since they often feel they are left in the dark. Every man at some point in his life claims he cannot understand women. Fortunately a man does not have to understand a woman in order to date one.

Thoughts versus Visual

I have shared that men and women are different. Besides obvious physical differences, women conceptualize more than men and are turned on mentally by thinking about the ideal man and ideal date. Men are visual and auditory and are affected by their surroundings. Ever wonder why there are no nude video arcades for women? There is no market.

Fantasies:

Fantasies are mental pictures of unreal conditions. Fantasies are fed by images and experiences in the real world, but the mind is free to add its own interpretation and meaning. Men are less prone to fantasy because they have sufficient visual stimulation and being oriented visually and auditorially they respond with interest and arousal. Women tend to develop fantasies internally and although the grist for the fantasy may be a real world condition or something they have seen or heard their minds develop a complex image of even dangerous proportions. I am going to posit a proposition for future study. Men fantasize with their eyes open. Women fantasize with their eyes closed.

Romance:

Thoughts of romance are different for men and women. Perhaps Oscar Wilde best summarizes the difference, *"Men want women to be their first love, women want men to be their last."* That is a flip way to describe romance. We need to dig deeper. Romantic stories, the ones to which women are addicted and men discard, are about giving oneself completely to the hero of the story who has swum the widest river, climbed the highest mountain, and gone through the lowest depths of the earth and prevailed while returning to the arms of the one woman for whom he did the feats and defeated all the demons.

Comfort Zone:

Everyone needs a comfort zone where their thoughts can go and they can be at peace. For men this is more likely to be a visual place and may involved action such as hunting and fishing. For a woman this place may be in the mind, or what Winnie the Pooh called "My happy place."

Safety and Protection:

A man must actively provide safety and protection. A woman must feel safe and protected.

Fear of Pregnancy:

Until there is a marriage, a woman has to worry about pregnancy with parental and social approbation along with the possibility that she may have to have and raise the child alone because the father may desert her.

I promised to get to Romeo and Juliet. Before they met, Juliet went out with Brutus, a local hero and big powerful guy who all the girls thought was masculine and would be a great catch. Brutus was physically appealing with heavy muscles hiding the fact that his private parts had shriveled due to steroids. (This is a modern story after all.)

Juliet went out on her first date of her life with Brutus expecting to fall in love with a physical specimen and have a trophy man to hold up to her friends. Wrong motive.

Juliet Knew She Had a Bad Date When She Went Out with Brutus Because…

- Brutus was late.
- Brutus honked the car horn for her to come out without having the courtesy to come in and face the family.
- Brutus failed to open the car door for Juliet and instead shouted "jump in" through the window.
- Brutus brought a friend along in the back seat of the car.
- Brutus took Juliet to the bowling alley for greasy burgers and fries and then waved to his friends to come over.
- Brutus never stopped talking about his sexual prowess and past women conquests.
- Brutus flirted with the waitress and bar maid.
- Brutus got drunk—before dinner.
- Brutus told dirty jokes that would make a sailor blush and laughed alone at every one of them.
- Brutus thought that his noxious gases emanating from either end of his body was better than her perfume.
- Brutus thought his gas emissions were funny.
- Brutus did not have enough money to pay the bill.
- Brutus did not open the car door at the end and she was left to walk up the steps alone, which by this time she was thankful.

Why did Juliet go out with Brutus in the first place? Was it because she had heard his reputation and wanted to have a novel adventure? Was it because he was the football star on a top rated high school team?

Meanwhile Romeo thought the prettiest cheerleader he had ever seen would make a great first date. Romeo found out from friends that her name was Jezebel. Jezebel was sexy, wore short skirts, showed her cleavage for review of everyone, and flirted excessively. Romeo thought he would really like to go out with Jezebel and invited her out on a first date.

Romeo Knew He Had a Bad Date When He Went Out with Jezebel Because…

- Jezebel was not ready when he picked her up.

- Jezebel did not introduce him to family members.
- Jezebel was uncommunicative other than her ex, about whom she could never stop talking.
- Jezebel was emotional at perceived slights unknown to Romeo and cried.
- Jezebel complained about the food and the restaurant.
- Jezebel ordered the most expensive wine and dinner plate on the menu.
- Jezebel left Romeo at the table and sat with some friends she spotted.
- Jezebel got drunk—before dinner.
- Jezebel slapped Romeo for suggesting they go for a private walk.
- Jezebel flirted with other men.
- Jezebel confessed to being a wino and that she had a history of mental illness including thoughts of suicide.
- Jezebel opened the car door herself almost before Romeo stopped and ran up the walk and slammed the door.

So why did Romeo go out with Jezebel in the first place? Was it because she was hot in her miniskirt and low cut blouse? Was it because he was set up with friends laughing behind his back?

Romeo met Juliet who was cut from a different cloth. Juliet was beautiful without ostentation. Juliet was reserved, but funny. Juliet dressed sharply, but not for sex. Romeo decided his next date would be with Juliet.

Romeo Prepares for the Date with Juliet

Romeo decided he had to do things differently. He began working out to improve muscle tone. He went to a hair stylist instead of having his friend cut his hair in a misshapen mass. Romeo bought some new clothes that looked sharp with an Ivy League style button down dress shirt and khaki pants. Romeo replaced his cheap cologne with a more expensive variety and stopped sneezing himself. Romeo's confidence improved and his self-esteem soared. Romeo asked what types of movie Juliet liked, which restaurants she discussed, what she liked to do. Her even consulted with Juliet when he phoned her up to ask for the date.

Juliet Prepares for the Date with Romeo

Like all women, Juliet began to have anxiety attacks about what she would wear and how would she look. She thought her dresses might be a year out of style, but Romeo had no clue about what was in style. Juliet's mother told her men did not worry about style, just cleanliness, neatness, and looking sharp. Since Romeo asked what she liked to do, she knew they were not going to that awful bowling alley. She wisely selected a moderately priced restaurant with an ocean view. She didn't want to absorb all his hard earned cash. Juliet thought about changing her hair color and style, but again her mother came to the rescues and said, "Why do you think he asked you out in the first place?" Juliet said, "I don't know? Juliet's mother kindly offered that whatever she was wearing and however she looked when Romeo invited her was the best plan. Juliet's mother wisely said, "A first date is not the time to experiment."

Romeo and Juliet Date: Perfection Personified

On their first date Romeo made none of the mistakes Brutus had made and Juliet made none of the mistakes Jezebel had made. Romeo and Juliet were courteous, had good manners, listened to the other talk with limited active participation until it was their turn, showed good taste, ordered a moderate meal, did not order an alcoholic drink, and had eyes only for the other.

Romeo seemed to do everything right. He pursued Juliet despite their families being at war with each other, which displayed his intense desire for her. Romeo brought a flower, or at least in the film I saw. What kind of quality date is Juliet looking for from Romeo? There are certain universal traits that are important to any Juliet. What about Romeo? Juliet had qualities that endeared her to Romeo. She defended his actions to all comers. She fought for him and his ideals. She kept secrets. What do you want from Juliet on your dates? Juliet was impressed and was ready to put Brutus in the rearview with Brutus's friend.

A Real Date
- Romeo arrived on time bringing flowers and Juliet was ready.
- Juliet introduced Romeo to her family who shook his

hand, beamed approval at his cleanliness, and gasped at the exquisite bouquet.

- On leaving her home, Romeo let Juliet go out first, closed the door and placed his hand at the small of her back as a first gesture or protection and affection.
- Romeo opened the car door for Juliet and made sure she was comfortable before gently closing it.
- They were alone, just the two, no friends in sight.
- Romeo took Juliet to a romantic restaurant overlooking the ocean and held her chair for her to be seated.
- Neither one wanted alcohol, although Romeo did ask Juliet what she wanted to drink.
- They ordered meals with modest portions and there were no noxious gases or anti-social sounds.
- Juliet never left the table and they engaged in a stimulating conversation without bringing up ex's, dates, or conquests.
- Romeo was attentive to Juliet's wants and needs. He asked what she was going to order and then remembered the order and placed it along with his. He asked if she would like desert and when she said no thanks, he did not order any either.
- Juliet was having so much fun she agreed to a walk in the well lit park.
- They kissed once for a few short seconds.
- Romeo returned her home, opened the car door, walked her to the door hand in hand and gave her a second goodnight kiss.
- They both thought they were in love from the beginning.

Kissing

When to kiss is a judgment call, or maybe better put it is an emotional call. Consider all collected evidence of how many boys or girls you believe your date has kissed.

A good kisser does not try to destroy the lips of the other person, but softly kisses the lips lightly parting the lips and actively but slowly moving the lips. That is a romantic kiss and not salacious or sex driven kisses that can grate teeth and swell the lips. I put kissing after the second and subsequent dates on purpose, but there is nothing wrong with a short kiss or two on the first date.

Getting Familiar

Holding hands is a natural sign of approval and affection. This starts the intimacy process and shows trust and confidence in a partner. A second or third kiss begins the intimate progression to eventual sex. Pressing not only lips, but bodies together is a shared intimacy that begins to stimulate imaginations.

Caressing is the next step toward sexual union and by this time, hopefully there have been several dates. Clothing is still a boundary so that things do not go too far, but definitely there is sexual expression and tenderness leading to more.

In western society the greater burden for stopping the advancement to sex is on the woman. It is natural for men to feel they must be the aggressor and that they are indicating their manliness by pressing for more. Unless a man is ready to face rape charges, he will respect the woman stopping him and saying no.

Women though are in a quandary and find it hard to decipher what the man is doing. The woman fears that stopping him will cause her to lose her ideal partner. By not stopping him the man may take advantage of her weakness and complete the sexual union without regard to the potential consequences including pregnancy. A woman can signal I want to do it, but am afraid of getting pregnant. I will discuss options in a later chapter.

Family Background

Family backgrounds, commonalities, and economic status often determine the likehood of one person asking the other for a date. In the past only the boy was expected to ask, but now the girl can take more of an initiative and suggest they go out together without the past title of bad girl.

Treatment of Opposite Sex

Dating is the time to see how a person treats someone of the opposite sex. Does the man show good manners and want to meet the family, open doors for her, hold her hand casually, kiss her tenderly, and take her wishes into account? Is this a shared experience or a one-man or woman show? Does the man or woman get out of control in public places?

How does the dating partner talk about the other person to friends and what filters back to the partner? Some corrections may be required when talking together about what others have said.

Respect Assessment

Respect assessment is the follow on to how the person treats the other sex. How do they treat third parties besides themselves? How do they talk about parents and family? How do they treat children and babies both physically and verbally? What kind of pedestal have they erected for you, if they have erected one at all?

Chapter 7

The Five C's of a Relationship

I LIKE THE IDEA of five categories starting with the letter "C" that define relationships and are necessary for solidifying the present relationship as well as working toward the next stage. These five "C's" are compatibility, commitment, communication, comfort, and caring.

Compatibility

Compatibility is an elusive term. Right fit is probably more meaningful. Both terms are about sharing experiences, sharing expectations, sharing dream, and sharing intentions. Shared experiences establish a bond. The more shared experiences that are favorable, the stronger the bond and memories that are difficult if not impossible to discard.

Sharing expectations is more of an adventure. Questions have to be asked and answered in a loving way of course. This does not have to be an interrogation. Questions can be asked and answered one at a time. A cute baby in a stroller passes by. "What do you think of having children? Do you like babies? How many kids would you like to have?" All natural questions flowing from the moment. Sharing dreams is opening up oneself with your vision, sharing, and finding out the partners ambitions, goals, and career ideas.

Intentions are more difficult to decipher. Often the other person has paid only limited attention to such thoughts of the future. He or she has probably never verbalized them. This then is virgin territory and an interesting adventure. The result though can determine how serious the other person is about the relationship and a future together. Where do you see us in six months, one year, three years?

There are a lot of serious topics to be addressed with your partner. Besides the ones mentioned, what about lifestyles, hobbies, finances, religion, political beliefs, and vacation destinations. Throughout the entire process you will not only gauge compatibilities, but determine areas for future discussion, future decisions, or future compromise. Understand that not everything has to fit and that interest may be added with some differences. I used to tell everyone I came from a divided family. My dad was a Democrat and my mother was a Republican.

Political discussions, however, improved my sense of history as they both watched political conventions and discussed the daily news. Many couples who seem to be complete opposites in personal tastes and affiliations can still create a healthy relationship and long term marriage. My mom and dad did. I could go through all the lists I prepared for this book, the nine forms of intelligence, the goal setting, and qualities and I would never put these two together, but the fit was dynamic. That is why I would never put my trust in Chemistry.com, Match.com, or any other match making mechanism. The glue holding everything together is Christ for the Christian, God for the Jew, prayer, and church/synagogue attendance.

Commitment

The tickets were purchased, the tickets are punched, you are now ready to get on board. In the Christian culture, commitment usually comes without having slept together or moved in together, though these bounds are loosening as each year goes by. Having your mother invite your boyfriend for Christmas or Easter dinner is a strong indicator to the boy that he is being accepted into the family and that you are no longer afraid to keep him separate from your family life. You are giving him a lifeline and bringing him in from the cold. The same applies to the boy's family and the rewards for both are extra gifts and extra food.

Of course sitting with each other at church and in Sunday School are strong indicators to each of not being ashamed of the other in public and a sign to others that they are excluded from the two person circle.

Exclusivity is important. The plain truth is there comes a time to decide you are ready to share the rest of your life with a mate. Commitment to a relationship means a pledge of allegiance to spend money, share time, find space, seek the other's company, and plan for the future. If the relationship becomes one sided, it will collapse. Monitor and balance the relationship as to who pays attention to whom and are things shared fairly and equally.

Communication

Communication skills include both verbal and physical indicators. The boy/man will face the greatest challenge for him in this realm, so girls/women please help. The boy/man will feel threatened, judged, and even insulted by bringing up problems or discussing the issues. Commitment is possible only by understanding at least a small part of each other and what the other wants and needs. Just as the need is great to communicate during sex, the need is great to communicate in a relationship. We have four C's of a relationship, so why not four P's for communication. The four P's are:

Problems:

Problems do not get solved on their own because each has a false sense of security and each has a different idea of the outcome. The longer there are issues that disturb you, the greater the chances of having them poison the well of love. You may show resentment, displeasure, and irritation at your partner and he or she cannot fathom what is going on with you. Mistrust, uncertainty, and fear of consequences of that little talk are viruses that are ready to take over the whole relationship.

It is best to tackle one problem at a time, especially if you have made a list of them. The list is good. Just don't throw it all at once. When discussing a problem area, make eye contact. Reading the look of surprise, pursed lips, and hurt expression will tell you how fast or slow to take the conversation. But take it you must. Don't postpone it---again!

Eye contact is important to show you believe in the person and are interested not only in getting across your point, but in listening to what they have to say. Eye contact is a sign of respect and communicates trust.

Positives:

Keep the relationship fresh. If it seems you are in a rut, you are. Do something different that you have ever done in your relationship. Take her to Disneyland to explore the child in her. Try something neither one of you have done before, though it would be a good idea to consult about sky diving or bunji jumping. Every date should have you meet as if for the first time in clean sharp clothes, well groomed face, and shined shoes, unless going to the beach in which case dress nicely and wear a nice bathing suit.

Look for the bright side of things and compliment the things that are attractive to you and work for you. Complaining, whining, asking how great you look, or criticizing over time will all destroy a relationship. No one wants to marry a nag. Humor is especially welcome, picking up on the others conversation or lines and making a funny comment are endearing. When the conversation is the toughest, laugh.

Don't take disagreement personally. This is hard for everyone, but it is not just about you, it is about the other person and the relationship.

Protection:

Protection of feelings is as critical as physical protection. Unless you are congenital twins, the biorhythms are different, feelings have been encultured in a different family or context, issues dealt with in one family are not handled the same way by your family model. Being prepared to fight for the one you love is important, but if the issue is out of hand let the cops handle it. Ask someone to call 911. This is not a flight idea, but one that is more protective than you can be on your own unless you are Chuck Norris or a Ninja. Even then they get help. A friend of mine defended the honor of his girlfriend and was shot for it. Better to have the cops do the shooting of the perpetrator. Of course there are situations where the only thing to do is fight. Make sure the girlfriend sprints away at the first available opportunity unless she is a Ninja too.

Preparation:

Preparation for a future together entails a lot identification of needs that I will help you with soon, of compromises that need to be made, of serious projections of time and space. This is sometimes the point where the male will run for cover. Do not fear. If he/she loves you he/she will apologize and return.

Comfort

Comfort does not mean passive acceptance of everything in the relationship. The term comfort incorporates trust in the other person's decisions, whereabouts, and predilections. A person can go insane wondering what the other one is doing right now, where are they really, who are they with? Anxiety insipiently slides into the mind and imaging the worst takes over until the mind is bent and trust is ready to explode into distrust. If that is a constant crisis for you, the answers are either to get engaged and married now, or see a pastor, if a Christian or a therapist if not. Anxiety leads to suffering as Yoda would tell us in Star Wars and "suffering leads to pain, to the dark side." The crux of the problem is also that smothering your partner with your insecurities, anxieties, and jealousy will harm the relationship. The bottom line is if you don't trust me, I don't need you.

Be reasonable. Discuss where you are going, who will be with you, and what you are doing. Be careful. Too much going out with friends or going places without the partner are a sign to him or her that something else is going on and he or she had better track you down. I would. Remember you are not trying to change the person you love at this point, oh well, let's face you do want to see a change. Now is the time to change the other person and have them conform to your expectations and you to theirs.

"Sex is the glue to hold a relationship together, but are you ready for that yet." Follow the old rule, never go to bed angry.

Caring

Caring is a broad category that includes sharing during the communication process, concern for the other person in the relationship, empathy, and understanding.

Sharing is not easy for everyone. A lot depends on family background and interaction in the past with parents. Some families find it natural to share, while others have a hard time. Individuals even in families that share may be selfish. Now that they are in a relationship they must open up to the other person and reveal not only their thoughts, but their thought processes. That can be difficult. Caring is about working with each other without accusations or blame. Caring like the rest of a relationship is centered on the other person, not you.

Concern for the health, mental and spiritual, as well as physical is part of caring for the other. Concern not only is oriented on the other person, but is a feeling about the status of the other. When one is sick or injured, I have seen and heard the immediate concern of the other expressed and have seen how they will do anything to assist their relational partner. This bodes well for the future marriage of the couple. Concern for the mental conditions of the partner is important, since it means one wants to get past an argument or anger over something the partner has done that offended sensibilities, but which must be overcome internally by your own mental acuity and toughness. Concern for the spiritual situation of the partner is the greatest concern and may require patience and prayer.

Empathy and understanding are closely related, but there are some differences. Empathy is the ability to put oneself in the shoes of the other person and leads to understanding their motivations and actions. Fitting ourselves into our partners position is not easy to do, because each person comes from a different family, environment, and background that are filters or blocks to full empathy and understanding. The best we can do is approximate what the other person means or does and then seek an explanation in a caring way from them as to why they did something and what their overall motivations may have been.

Christianity, Jewish Faith, or Other Religion

The best glue is actually Christianity, the Jewish Faith, or other religious beliefs with common goals, common approaches to sex, and common views of faithfulness and marriage. The Christian is free to add a sixth letter, "C", to the relationship category for Christianity.

Chapter 8

Sustaining the Premarital Relationship
With or Without Sex

PREMARITAL RELATIONSHIPS ARE DEFINED here as a boy or man going together with a girl or woman for more than three months and having had several dates. A long term relationship has developed with emotional capital now invested in sustaining the relationship. The longer the investment is made, the greater the emotional capital. If there is an investment over two years, that relationship should remain solid and a powerful continuing attraction. There is no need to date anyone else. Your mate for life has been found. Premarital relationships can take years to arrive at engagement and marriage, especially when started in high school. By marriage the relationship has been assailed by one or both partners considering whether to have sex, or to abstain until marriage, by seemingly everyone else having sex, and by vulnerabilities that Satan throws at us to exploit our own desires and weaknesses.

The strong and wise couple will resist outside forces and concentrate on building their relationship internally until they are certain they have the money, jobs, or resources to start a family. That is usually between five and seven years out of high school. In the modern world this time is essential for completing college, completing two years of military service, and starting a career.

The wise counselor will affirm that the best relationship concentrates on the other party and not one's own sexual and emotional needs. Both parties must be in agreement on things such as length of engagement, date of wedding, and sexual intercourse before marriage. Chapter 10 demonstrates that there is no need for guilt in having sex before marriage, but the emphasis is on agreement after discussion taking into account a right relationship together as part of God's plan and not our own. There is no need to prove sexual competency before marriage. The purest and best sex is that which has mutual agreement after prayer and trusting the other party to do the right thing regardless of the timing. In fact the most powerful sexual aphrodisiac is faithfulness mixed with loyalty.

God has a Plan, Don't Mess with It!

In the Book of Jonah, the Bible says that God had a plan for Jonah, but Jonah tried to hide from God's plan. Look at the terrible storm that rocked the boat where Jonah was hiding from God and God's plan. Think about Jonah being tossed overboard and sinking to the bottom of the sea in the belly of a great fish (whale). Don't mess with God's plan. If God has put you together with someone for more than two years, you can be certain that God meant for you to have this relationship. Don't mess with it?

> *For I know the plans I have for you," declares the Lord,*
> *"plans to prosper you and not to harm you, plans to*
> *give you hope and a future. Then you will call upon me*
> *and come and pray to me, and I will listen to you."*
> *Jeremiah 29:11-12.*

Relational Partner

The term "significant other" conjures up living together, so I have had to invent a new term that I call "relational partner." Relational partners are in a firm and continuing, probably abiding, relationship, but are not living together or necessarily having sexual intercourse. Relational partners are committed though to making the relationship work with the future goal of marriage in the near or longer term future. The secular term, "significant other," is used to define a living together arrangement and having sex without being married (cohabitation). That has its own set of conditions that are outside the purview of this book.

Seven Practical Problematic Relational Experiences

Doubt:

Everyone is beset by doubts: doubts that prayers are heard, doubt that a relationship will survive, doubt about ourselves, doubt about the relational partner, and doubt about the future of the relationship.

First, get it in your mind that after more than two years with a relational partner, the odds are highly stacked entirely in your favor that the relationship will end in marriage. I still like the idea of emotional capital being invested and excluding others from the dating process that a true working relationship demands.

Second, deal with the doubt in a loving way with your relational partner without accusations. There are going to be times in a relationship mainly prior to engagement and marriage that the actions of the partner are suspect in your eyes and need to be confronted.

Third, explain the doubt by how it makes you feel and don't lay the heavy guilt on your partner. This is the healthy way to take care of things. By explaining your feelings about how the partner operates in public gives both a chance to come to an agreement about fixing it.

Fourth, take baby steps to wall off you and your partner from others. How about pruning the friends of the opposite sex on your social networking Internet page and asking your partner to do the same? How about communicating to others at work that you are committed to a relational partner and asking your relational partner to do the same? How about adding a nice picture of you and your relational partner together to your social networking site? How about making sure when you are invited to a party with mixed sexes that you invite your relational partner or tell your partner and the host/hostess that you are not going because your relational partner would be excluded?

The way to do this is to make the first move and tell the relational partner what you are doing. Some partners do take more than a hint, however, so gently broach the subject of the partner doing similar things. Expectations are in our own minds until they are communicated.

Fear:

Fear like doubt is a universal human trait that is amplified the more we give in to it. Fear is feeling invading our thoughts that the future may be uncertain. When so much is invested in a relationship, fear of opening up ourselves to our relational partner and expressing our fears becomes an obstacle to the relationship itself. Fear begets worry and worry begets fretting until we are sick from something that is easily cured.

I cannot just say get rid of fear. Fear is a powerful emotion. Understand that if you are having fears, so is your relational partner. Fear is essential to protecting the self from outside forces. You do not fear alone. Your relational partner has their own set of fears. I can tell you how to get rid of the strongest fears in a relationship.

First, communicate the basis for the fear together. An example might be, unless we have sexual intercourse, I am afraid that you will not marry me. That is a valid fear in most long term relationships and it gets back to the amount of emotional capital invested in the relationship. Your relational partner almost guaranteed has the same fear.

Second, agree on future goals and time frames for further commitment.

Third, engagement is the next step to getting rid of fear in the life of a couple. Engagement is like stepping out from the shadow of fear into the light of major commitment. Even before engagement, there is no problem with considering the date for a future marriage and then preparing for it by saving money, building assets, and planning the wedding. The power of the diamond engagement ring is it shines out to everyone that your relationship is certainly exclusive without you having to explain it to the stupid horde. Fears residing in both partners dissipate rapidly with the engagement ring on the finger of the female relational partner.

Impatience:

I will extol the virtues of patience as one of the foundation stones that form the seven building blocks of granite in the next section. Impatience is easy to define as lack of patience, but it stems from a deeper well. We are a results oriented society and expect instant gratification. Impatience leads us to do things on the spur of the moment and thoughts of revenge come to mind for something we believe our relational partner many have done or committed without a shred of evidence or even talking to them. It happened to me where I was the victim. I know it can happen to you.

Rest on God's word and plan for living, do not dwell on the things that make us impatient. I use the word rest, because the rested soul and spirit is one that reposes in the will of God and takes comfort from that ever living fountain.

Mistrust:

Mistrust is the opposite of trust much like impatience is the opposite of patience. Relationships are always and constantly tested with the potential for mistrust at every turn. Mistrust is amplified by distance apart and times separated. That is almost a formula for mistrust.

Countering mistrust is not just words of reassurance that nothing is going on. As with all seven practical problems, communication about every situation, every place to which the relational partner is going, every associate of the partner, every event attended without the other partner and every situation in which one finds themselves should be discussed and explained freely in order to assuage the sensitivities of the other. Avoidance of the people, places, and events that the partner finds a problem is the best way to take care of mistrust. Calling, texting, or emailing are the only ways to compensate for distance and time away from the other.

Physical Wants:

Physical wants are the most difficult problem for a relationship and this takes a lot of prayer for the requisite resoluteness afforded by faith, hope, love, patience, and trust. Physical wants run the gamut from holding hands to sexual intercourse. God wants couples to have happiness, yet the physical nature of human beings seems to get in the way. Chapter 10 deals with ways of coping with sex before marriage for those who have experienced it.

The central message of this book is that a couple can be happy without sexual intercourse as long as they invest the rest of their emotions in each other and build a wall around themselves. In fact we are told that increased doubts, fear, and mistrust in a relationship are caused by having premarital sex and then worrying about what the other person is doing when we are not there, or worrying about the consequences of having sex such as pregnancy. Kissing and petting are normal and necessary to a healthy relationship. Sexual intercourse is special and if the couple can refrain until marriage, the marriage is much stronger for the wait. The other message is that if there is premarital sexual intercourse, the couple can still find happiness without guilt that it is against the Bible.

Sharing:

Sharing is difficult for men, a necessity for women. Women are more likely to experience a sense of inner fulfillment when they share their thoughts in a relationship. Talking about problems, is a woman's way of sharing. Unfortunately men often take discussion of problems either as a critique of them personally, or as a reflection on their judgment. One of the most frustrating things for a woman to endure is the lack of attention paid to their thoughts and needs. When a man is perceived as failing to listen or is preoccupied with his work, a woman takes it as rejection and suffers a loss of personal esteem

Men must listen actively and not look for a solution. Often in sharing through discussion the woman simply wants approval and empathy, not a solution. Men have a hard time deciphering a woman as a result and want to make a statement or judgment that he thinks will solve the problem.

Vulnerability:

The strength of a relationship is judged by personal vulnerabilities. Vulnerabilities are exposed when couples are apart. Vulnerabilities are personality driven, but prayer controlled, so an understanding of each other is critical in assessing the potential for vulnerabilities along with the amount of prayer needed.

The longer and stronger the relationship, the less likely vulnerabilities will surface even by separation or a time out. Military spouses have to face a year at a time of separation. Support groups, church groups, a personal circle of friends experiencing the same separation sustain military spouses and make the time go by faster without exposing vulnerabilities. There should be more such groups for men and women like the military.

Pray for personal strength and for the strength of the relational partner when separated even for a day. A strong relationship can sustain breaks for two or three months as long as both are trying to deal with things like work, duty, and preparation for the joint future.

Religious Centered Relationship

Christian and/or Jewish couples in a relationship consider God's plan for their lives as the building blocks and prayer as the cement holding them together. When the focus is on God, the attractive things of this world fade in comparison. What are the elements of God's Plan?

I give you the best made and formed eight blocks of granite you can find for building your temple of holy matrimony. A hundred more could be given, but these eight set the foundation that will not be rocked by the storms of life. As the Bible said, the wise man built his house upon a rock.

Seven Building Blocks Made of God's Granite

Faith, hope, and love are the first three great blocks of granite God gives us to emotionally deal with the world. Patience and perseverance are two more blocks added to this foundation, but they require a lot of prayer to polish them.

I have a new practical quote for you taken from a quote by John Quincy Adams: *"Patience and perseverance have a magical effect before which difficulties disappear and obstacles vanish."* This is a powerful quote because making difficulties disappear and obstacles vanish is no easy feat. Let me amplify that quote with one of my own: *"Patience, whether in love, business, or war wins all, perseverance gets us there."* Patience is the state of mind and perseverance is the active road grader that removes the difficulties and obstacles in its path.

Faith:

There are a lot of verses in the Bible that deal with faith. Other than the love chapter in Corinthians for which a poem I wrote is included in this book, I have two favorite faith quotes from the Bible that relate to couples in a relationship.

1. I tell you the truth, if you have faith as small as a mustard seed, you can say to this mountain, 'Move from here to there' and it will move. Nothing will be impossible for you."

Matthew 17:20 (NIV)

Sermons have been written on having mustard seed size faith. The mustard seed is a very small seed indeed. Faith is conditioned by prayer and calling on God. If we have the faith, God moves the mountain.

2. ...*it is by faith you stand firm.* 2 Corinthians 1:24 (NIV)

Standing firm in a relationship means standing with your relational partner scanning the horizon, preparing for the winds that will surely come, and defeating the outside forces that seek to destroy the relationship. I always loved the song, "I shall not be moved." Faith has roots, just like the tree beside the waters in the song.

When I was sent as an Army Attaché to Moscow in 1983, my wife was trained to stand firm with me protecting my flanks and back, looking for potential counteragents while I accomplished the various collection missions assigned to me. My wife stood with me in critical situations. I had faith in her. That is the way a relationship should work. Standing together and having faith in each other to do what is in their best interests while protecting the partner.

Hope:

Hope is one of the three things that last forever (abide), according to 1 Corinthians 13:13. The other two are faith and love. We have thrilled to the phrase "hope beyond hope." We know beyond all shadow of a doubt that something was meant to be and so we invest our hope in the thing we know was meant to be and succeed against all odds.

Love:

According to 1 Corinthians 13:13, the greatest of faith, hope, and love is love. I believe in eternal love. I believe the greatest capacity in the human soul is love. Love does conquer all. Love means acceptance of the other person regardless of how we found them or what they have become. Love means that we submit our prayers, supplications, and thoughts on behalf of someone. Love means never having to say you are sorry, just disappointed. Then love goes on forever.

Patience:

I have found that patience is the virtue for which we have the least patience. We have all heard of the patience of Job. We have also heard the story of Jacob working seven years for the hand of Rachel in marriage and then his future father-in-law saying he had to work another seven years. Fourteen years of patience to get married to the one you love is on the long end of my scale, but Jacob had patience beyond the norm.

Perseverance:

Perseverance is going against the odds and overcoming obstacles. In a relationship perseverance is the force that continues to strive in the face of what others may say on a course of action toward an objective despite discouragement. All relationships require hard work both to maintain the relationship and to move forward toward marriage and happiness. Work on a relationship is rewarded in the end with a happy life.

Truth:

In the courtroom we raise our hand and "Solemnly swear to tell the truth, the whole truth, and nothing but the truth." Once in a relationship there should be an independent body or person that makes couples swear to tell the whole truth. Truth sometimes hurts, but it beats telling whatever comes second after the truth (lying, deception, clever avoidance, and other verbal tricks). Truth can cut to the quick if something hurtful has happened, but the wound can quickly heal where there is a clean cut. Truth can inspire. Truth can correct. Truth builds both hope and trust.

A lie may have a motivation that is unknown to the partner who discovers or thinks there has been a lie. Before judging too harshly the motivation must be discovered. What I am saying is do not throw out the relationship on one or two lies. Get over it quickly when discovered and move on to productive activities. A pattern of lies, however, means the entire relationship is in doubt and must be assessed by the partner who discovers the pattern of lies.

Trust:

What the couple does and how each partner acts when they are together forms the basis for a trusting relationship. Reports of fidelity when apart reinforce trust. I do not believe where there is love that trust can be broken. Downgraded for a time maybe, but not broken as long as the truth is told and forgiveness is quick to the rescue.

Seven Strengthening Components of God's Cement

Cement is composed of strengthening agents, in addition to the main sand and gravel materials used in buildings. God's cement is similarly an amalgam of strengthening agents that are mixed, with patience and perseverance as the sand and gravel. I have identified seven strengthening agents.

Bible Study:

Bible study is wonderful when shared together either just the two of you reading to each other, or being in a church sponsored group. But beware the Bible study leader and the agenda the leader may have that runs counter to the true word of God. Not all Bible study leaders are qualified to lead and not all Bible studies are created equally. Dwell on the word of God and not on the agenda. Desert the Bible study group that runs counter to your conscience and twists the word. Know the qualifications of the text writer, if one is used in the study, and learn about his or her agenda as well.

As a deacon, I went through this process and left Bible studies with ulterior motives. I formed my own bible study group and selected amplifying texts written by people I could trust.

Church/Synagogue Attendance:

Church selection is like selecting a Bible study. Find the best fit for both of you in the relationship and regularly attend church. Not only is church attendance and listening to the word of God being preached a salve to the soul, church is the best date one can share. Church attendance together signals strong commitment to a relationship and obedience to God. Attending together signals to others that the relationship is in God's hands, do not disturb.

Christian Association:

Associating with Christians beats associating with club or bar patrons. The chances of dealing with worldly people in a Christian setting are greatly reduced.

Religious Fellowship:

Religious fellowship offers at least the chance for talking with similarly motivated and seeking couples and leaders with a chance for them to pray for you and your personal relationship with each other.

Religious Leaders:

Religious leaders: pastors, priests, rabbis, deacons, and elders are available for consultation on issues affecting a relationship. At least you know the advice or prayer is religiously oriented and not secular pap.

Pray Alone:

In those quiet times, pray for you, your relational partner, and your relationship both with them and with God.

Pray Together: Besides being a good time to hold hands, praying together strengthens both relational partners and the relationship. The more this happens it is like putting another coat of protective varnish on a precious piece of wood.

Seven Areas of Commitment to the Relational Partner

There are seven key areas of commitment to the relational partner that condition our concerns and temper our responses. As with most of my lists these are in alphabetical order.

Empathy:

Empathy is putting oneself in the shoes of the other person to look from their perspective on the world. I understand that this is a difficult thing to do and it does take practice, because up to the relationship we have been thinking of us and believe the other person should be thinking of us, but empathy is a quality that every relationship must have.

A new CBS television series in 2010, "The Undercover Boss," has made a major impact on communicating the importance of empathy in business relationships. In the series one of the top bosses of a franchise or company is placed disguised and undercover in the role of a basic worker just starting to learn the business. Within the first day the undercover boss begins to understand the difficulties confronting their hires and changes the entire business model to focus on the worker. Millions watch as the boss stumbles around trying to comprehend multitasking roles, takes forever to make a sandwich, and dumps the trash. That is empathy.

The best movies are the ones in which we can empathize with the hero or heroine as they are attacked or persevere through hardships and relationships. Think of each couple as writing their own script. Now be sure to include empathy for each other.

Future:

Committing to a relationship means committing to a future together. Plans need to be made about the destination of the premarital relationship which is engagement and marriage followed by the potential for children and all that child bearing and child rearing entails.

Leadership and Responsibility:

Please understand what I am saying under leadership and responsibility. The Bible sets out the rule of relationships in marriage between a husband and wife. I am emphatically telling you that like a team practices for the main game, the same must be done in a premarital relationship. By extension backwards to premarital relationships, the same principles apply. Let's take a look at leadership and responsibility in premarital relationships and marriage. Admonishment in Ephesians is first to the wives and then to the husband (by extension back to the man and woman in a premarital relationship).

The position of women in a relationship (Wives): " *22 Wives, submit yourselves to your own husbands as you do to the Lord. 23 For the husband is the head of the wife as Christ is the head of the church, his body, of which he is the Savior. 24 Now as the church submits to Christ, so also wives should submit to their husbands in everything."* (NIV) "Everything" is all encompassing and leaves no room to wiggle.

We are not talking slavery and servitude as in a master slave relationship. We are talking leadership, guidance, and direction with love. These three components require consultation, communication, and consistency. Pity the relational male partner (husband) not consulting or considering his female partner's (wife's) position, arguments, and wishes.

The position of men in a relationship (Husbands): **"25 Husbands, love your wives, just as Christ loved the church and gave himself up for her 26 to make her holy, cleansing[a] her by the washing with water through the word, 27 and to present her to himself as a radiant church, without stain or wrinkle or any other blemish, but holy and blameless. 28 In this same way, husbands ought to love their wives as their own bodies. He who loves his wife loves himself. 29 After all, no one ever hated their own body, but they feed and care for their body, just as Christ does the church— 30 for we are members of his body. 31 "For this reason a man will leave his father and mother and be united to his wife, and the two will become one flesh." 32 This is a profound mystery—but I am talking about Christ and the church. 33 However, each one of you also must love his wife as he loves himself, and the wife must respect her husband."** (NIV)

Responsibilities do not stop there. According to Ephesians 5, the husband is to cherish his wife. Cherish means tenderness, love and affection toward the wife. Value her above all possessions. Men, I am talking to you again. Love requires care and feeding, warm demonstrations of love in the relationship, and telling her you love her. Don't forget the physical side of demonstrating love including kissing, touching, rubbing, and eventually sexual intercourse as the most intimate of the physical forms of affection. Men, do not let the physical forms of affection be the only way to demonstrate it. Women need mental and spiritual feeding.

A male partner is told in I Peter 3:7 to honor the female partner. Of course Peter is talking to husbands here, but remember, we are extending the concept back as I believe God would tell us to premarital relationships. The concept of honor means a wide range of human behavior including respect, courtesy, consideration, and emotional support. This especially applies in public, since the female relational partner is now part of who you are. Never cut down the woman with caustic or sarcastic remarks to anyone else or in public. You in fact are cutting yourself. Calling her "stupid" makes you stupid.

A final term is of use here and that is "forbearance." Ephesians 4:32 teaches, "*forbear one another.*" Forbearance means patience. It means controlling your tempers and not physical abusing anyone. Forbearance means not berating the other to make them feel inferior. A relationship is to uphold the other, protect the other, and have patience with the other no matter the time or attention it takes.

Love:

Love as a commitment is unconditional. Love is giving all you have to give. Love goes beyond taking a risk to the realm of "I do not care about the risk." Love defines us and shapes us.

Motivation:

Motivation is purposeful thinking to move toward a goal. Motivation to become married means that all the right steps will be taken, a support base prepared in the premarital stage, and the drive to succeed is now multiplied by at least two, more if there is a baby on the way.

Selflessness:

Selflessness like love is a giving commitment. Selflessness means we are satisfied the options have been considered and we now submit to each other for the greater good of the relationship. This is not giving in to the whims of the other. This is seeking a positive outcome after communication and understanding that the female wishes have been considered and the male is now responsible for the exercise of the proper tasks on behalf of the partnership.

Understanding:

Understanding differs from empathy in that we may learn to have empathy, but need to add perspective, to figure out why the relationship is what it is and why the other person in the relationship acts the way they do.

Chapter 9

Premarital Sex and Sex Education

PREMARITAL SEX IS A matter of prayer for the young religious couple. Comfort with morals, cultural standards, and Bible interpretation is the key. As already mentioned, sex is the glue that holds the long term couple together. The real problem is that one or both partners are inexperienced on their wedding night. Not knowing the right things to do, they stumble along and actually can have a miserable time until they communicate and practice together.

I want to make it clear that I am not advocating premarital sex. From my research, logic, and perceptions, however, I also want to make it clear that if premarital sex is performed between a loving couple, no guilt or shame should attach to them. Premarital sex is an intensely private discussion and decision for each couple.

Christian Views

Christian views on premarital sex vary widely and are often the subject of misinterpretation. Christian teachings against premarital sex arose with the Catholic Church and fundamentalists in the Middle Ages, leaving 1,500 years of previous history without preaching guilt and shaming the couple that has premarital sex.

The word *porneia* in the Greek, is used in many places in the Bible and was interpreted into English with the King James Bible with the word fornication; however, in Biblical Greek the word *porneia* meant sexual immorality or sexual perversion and did not refer to premarital sex. Sexual immorality is defined as having sex with prostitutes, taking multiple sex partners, and includes perversions that do not need to be mentioned here. No one could find me a case where this word is against premarital sex.

Biblical Views Interpretation and Misinterpretation

Premarital sex is not a sin and furthermore it is a way for the both partners to experience a deep and abiding love as one unit. There is nothing in the Bible that is against having sex before marriage, only misinterpretations by extreme conservatives. In every case of premarital sex in the Bible there is no punishment for the sexual act(s). The only penalty is the compensation to the father for the woman's change in status. Jesus never condemned premarital sex or even sexual orientation.

Sexual Principles in Reality

Sex is a Human Condition and Prerequisite to be Human:

All humans have sex whether with someone or on their own. If nothing else, virtually all women and men masturbate, even priests and pastors. (Now I know I am going to be threatened with stoning for sure.) Recent research found that masturbation is healthy and not the "threat of going blind" as some parents once taught.

Humans Fantasize about Sex:

All humans have fantasies involving sex. The issue then is controlling the fantasy and doing it mentally with the one you love.

Premarital Sex is Accepted and Virtually Universal in Modern Society:

Birth control pills changed the status of women. In surveys conducted in the United States the average age that a girl first has sex with someone is 17. Maybe we need to change our laws back to the age of 16 for consent. From the biblical perspective, as noted already, there is no prohibition of premarital sex. A large majority of men and women have premarital sex, even the moral majority. Now I have been added to another hit list.

In a short article news release by the Guttmacher Institute, a respected organization, a study by Lawrence B. Finer is mentioned and the headline of the article is "Premarital Sex has been Universal among Americans and has been for Decades." In the article it states, 9 in 10 women born even in the 1940's had premarital sex and 95% of women overall had premarital sex. [Source: http://www.guttmacher.org/media/nr/2006/12/19/index.html]

Now I am left with only 5% of the population wanting to stone me.

Guilt is not Necessary:

Sex is not dirty, but an act of giving and when done with someone the person loves the results are wonderful. Since everyone has sexual thoughts, why should anyone be guilty?

Sexual Communication is Key:

Everyone seems to be afraid to open themselves up to what they sexually desire. In a relationship, the partner needs to know your thoughts and whether he or she can meet the fantasies, desires, and needs of the other. Preferences and sexual activities need to be discussed and consideration given to the other's expression of love in a relationship.

Sex is Separate from Love:

Love is different from sex. Love includes a hierarchy of protection (physically or by declaration and intent), security (financial, cultural, understanding), sharing (household chores and jobs, thoughts, goods, and services), caring (wanting the best for the other person), desire (sexual and proximity), and loyalty (under all conditions or stresses of life). Sex is mental (fantasies) and physical (bodily contact) intimacy that is not only normal, but universal.

The Bible and Sex

Galatians 5:1 'For freedom Christ set us free; therefore keep standing firm and do not be subject again to a religious yoke of slavery."

This is a repudiation of the Jewish law from the Old Testament. Jesus never talked about sexual orientation. Nothing in the life and teachings of Jesus deals with sexual orientation. Jesus taught acceptance of ourselves and others as having equal value to God.

Premarital Sex - Not a Biblical Conflict

There is absolutely nothing in the Bible forbidding premarital sex. [**Source:** http://www.libchrist.com/bible/premaritalsex.html]

In Bible times young women were engaged based on a family financial deal. Sometime she never even met her husband until the wedding day. Once engaged families waited until the girl was 12.5 year old before they could marry. There was little dating, singles sexuality was never an issue.

In biblical times there was nothing wrong with a married man having as many wives as he could afford, concubines, and "common" prostitutes. Adultery was only wrong for a married women, since it violated her husband's property rights over her and his other wives or concubines.

David, who was said to walk with God, was chastised by God for pursuing Bathsheba and causing the death of her husband by instructing his generals to make sure and place him in the front lines of battle so he would be killed. Do you remember the son David and Bathsheba produced? It was King Solomon. David was forgiven by God. By the way, both David and Solomon had a large retinue of wives.

In Bible times men were masters, (daughters, wives, concubines, handmaidens, servants etc) and **if you wanted to have sex with one of his property, then you had to ask his permission.**

Some Concubines were war gifts to soldiers for fighting in battle. They would kill all the men and then divide up all the women to the fighting men. Some concubines were bought at auctions. Prostitutes rented themselves on a time-limited basis and were never considered an evil thing (common not temple prostitutes worshiping the fertility gods - idolatry was wrong not prostitution). It was better to buy a woman then rent one. Sexually repressive teachings that developed in the middle ages are still followed today based on repressive Christian traditions - out of ignoranceand having no biblical basis.

Judeo-Christian Perspective (Old Testament Passages)
Payment to a father for a virgin not engaged and having sex

Exodus 22:16 - 17, "If a man seduces a virgin who is not engaged, and lies with her, he must pay a dowry for her to be his wife. If her father absolutely refuses to give her to him, he shall pay money equal to the dowry for virgins."

Obviously this rarely applies today.

Payment for Rape

Neither the man nor woman is punished as long as payment is made. Deuteronomy 22:28 – 29 says, "If a man finds a girl who is a virgin, who is not engaged, and seizes her and lies with her and they are discovered, then the man who lay with her shall give to the girl's father fifty shekels of silver, and she shall become his wife because he has violated her; he cannot divorce her all his days."

There are a couple of important points concerning this passage: First, neither the man or woman is rebuked or punished for any sin (compare with Deut. 22). The man is required to seek marriage but can be refused by the father. The key here is that there is no punishment for the man and woman having sex. The punishment is for the change in value of the woman as bride. Also note that there is no law concerning the pre-marital sexuality of men or unbetrothed non-virgin women.

The passage in Deuteronomy refers to a rape not consensual pre-marital sex. In order to remedy this crime, the man must take the woman into his household and care for her. He cannot divorce her. The rape of a married or engaged woman carried the death penalty. The rape of a virgin who is not engaged carries a lesser penalty. And while the penalty may seem unjust by our culture's standpoint, the penalty was probably very just for that culture. Rape was a civil matter and not a criminal matter, unless the rapist did not accept the raped person into his household and care for her.

Deception, not Sex is Wrong

In Deuteronomy 22 there is a clear example of what happens to a woman who has had sex prior to her marriage but deceives her parents and husband into believing that she was a virgin and accepted money ("playing the harlot in her father's house") for her virgin status. Although the severe penalty for such a deception is stoning, the husband can show love, forgiveness and mercy.

There are two other examples of pre-marital sex in the OT. In Deut. 21:10 there is another case study of how a man is to handle a captive woman. If he desires her as a wife, he must follow the conditions and then sleep with her. If she is found pleasing, he has the option to marry her or he can send her away. The book of Esther also describes how Esther is brought into the King's household to become a part of the King's harem.

Practical View

If one is afraid of having a baby, one can have sex for twenty out of thirty days a month and practice abstinence the other ten days, use a condom, pull out before ejaculation, have oral sex, or ask the female to use a birth control measure such as the pill, diaphragm, coil, or other pregnancy prevention system. A woman has a fertile period only once per month. Catholics practice abstinence from sex during the day or so around the likely time of fertility.

Four Ways to Have Sex without Getting Pregnant

1. Follow the bouncing period.

Every thirty days more of less a woman has a period with blood discharge. A woman knows the time between periods and keep track on a calendar. An egg (ovum) is ready to be fertilized either a day before the period or a day after and lives without fertilization only 12 to 24 hours; however 48 hours is calculated in case there is more than one egg. Sperm that is introduced into the vagina, lives up to 5 days after intercourse, though the norm is only 2 days. Pregnancy is more likely to occur if intercourse is completed 2-3 days before ovulation or 2-3 days after ovulation. To be extra cautious, add three days more on either side. That makes five days before and 3 days after. The other 22 days are safe for sex without pregnancy. A woman's fertile time ("unsafe days" if she wants to prevent pregnancy) is thus about one-third of her cycle.

2. Birth Control System.

A condom, the pill, female condom, cervical cap, or IUD can be used to prevent pregnancy the entire time with less than a 99% chance of pregnancy.

3. Terminate Intercourse Before Ejaculation.

While this works, the intimacy is often too great and the act is consummated at least partially before the man realizes he is starting his discharge of bodily fluid.

4. Practice Oral Sex.

Oral sex is pleasurable for both partners with guidance from each as to what is most satisfying. Since oral sex is not as pleasing as vaginal intercourse, it can be a substitute if birth control methods are not used up to and just after the period. The taboos associated with oral sex are gone and practiced by a loving couple can be quite satisfying. Nothing takes the place of intercourse between a man and a woman and that is the basis for a long and happy life together.

Pleasure of Sex

By now you have either put down the book, burned it, or are continuing on with gasps and morbid curiosity. You also know why a pastor cannot write such a heresy. He would be stoned. The strongest union between a man and woman is sexual union. Sex is to be enjoyed. Even the Amish are more open to discussing sex than Baptists. Sex education has been around now for 20 years or so. Let's shed a little light on the pleasure of sex.

A young woman wrote in AdviseMen.com a short treatise on the "Top 5 Things Women Want from Their Man." The following is a summation of that short treatise, but the message is clear. Do the right things and you will keep your partner for life. Satisfaction is the name of the game. As the writer says, "…if implemented the right way. (these 5 things) will make your woman crazy for more every time." The reason I turned to this method of presentation, by the way, is that I am a man; therefore a woman writing would be more believable and effective. The order was not quite right, so I changed that and paraphrased the article except for direct quotes. I have also added some items from other sources.

Foreplay

We are told from other sources that a woman needs up to 20 minutes of sexual arousal in advance of the sex act. This is called foreplay. Senses need to be aroused, natural vaginal secretions can lubricate the love channel in preparation for penetration, and getting closer to the first orgasm (climax) means less stamina and withholding of ejaculation is needed by the male. Kissing, sucking on breasts, fondling the clitoris gently, and inserting one or two fingers into the vagina mimicking eventually penal penetration prepare the woman. A sure way is to play with the clitoris as discussed below. This is particularly important for young couples to understand, because believe it or not men think a woman should have an orgasm, just because he is having one. The first time you two may not get it right, but soon you will and both will be immensely satisfied. If lubrication is a problem, try one of the new sexual gels such as KY Intense.

Clitoris Concentration

The surest way to bring a woman to orgasm is to pay attention to the clitoris, that little soldier at the top of her labia standing out a little. Especially with first time sex, the man has no clue where to find it. Help him. A good deal of the nerve endings that supercharge the woman to climax are found there. If neglected, it can prevent the orgasm and mutual satisfaction. Lick the clit before penetration as part of foreplay and afterward if the woman has not achieved orgasm. As the article mentions, "Performing oral sex is one of the safest bets to use when concentrating on her orgasm, do it and do it often!"

Talk Dirty

Here I go offending Christian sensitivities again, but I have it on good authority that Christians who have a good sex life talk dirty in bed. Women love to hear what the man is going to do to them. It inspires the imagination. Mix in adoration and you have hit a home run! Guys, you know you like to talk dirty sometimes. Surprise! A woman loves to hear it, but only in bed, or in preparation for sex if you are going to do it somewhere else.

Communicate

Both the man and the woman need to communicate their desires. The only way to find out is to ask, both of you. Each woman and each man is unique. Maybe the man likes a little oral stimulation before the act of intercourse. Maybe he does not like before sex. Even just asking is a signal of love, attention, and affection. The woman will be turned on by your curiosity and desire to please.

Lasting Longer

The article states, "Women take longer than men, in fact, an average of 8 minutes longer, to reach the point of orgasm and all too often men are finishing way before that 8 minutes is up." There are solutions for this including the faithful KY lotions, pills for male endurance, vitamins, and other products from the pharmacy. Varying the tempo from fast at the beginning to slow and then taking a moderate rhythm is one technique. Pulling out entirely for a few second when the "rush" starts to develop and then starting slowly again is another technique. Having the woman on top and setting her own pace is a third technique.

As the AdviseMen.com article concludes, "It does not take an Adonis to satisfy a woman sexually, it just takes a little curiosity, effort and education."

Abortion and the Bible

An abortion is a personal choice with prayer and seeking God's guidance. If a child is unwanted, it would be a tragedy to bring it into the world. Of that I am convinced. I believe that in the case of rape, physical and mental health of the mother, and situations involving "unequal yoking" the pregnant girl has the right to decide.

No Prohibition of Abortion:

I am not making a case for or against abortion. I believe circumstances dictate the decision to abort.

There is flat out no passage in the Bible prohibiting abortion. Pro-life advocates led by pastors, evangelists, and radio/tv broadcasters, will take passages out of context beginning with "Thou shalt not kill," and then cite Psalms and Job where it talks about being in the mother's womb. But there is still no passage prohibiting abortion. "Kill" by the way is properly translated from the Greek as "murder," which involves a civil attack on an "innocent" human, not for self defense or termination of a fetus. God does not condemn abortion or support it. Christian leaders do the condemning.

King Solomon Can Be Viewed as on the Side of Abortion

I can make a much stronger case for abortion than against it by reading the whole Bible. Solomon can be deemed to support abortion with these words: *"Better the miscarriage than he, for it comes in futility and goes into obscurity; and its name is covered in obscurity. It never sees the sun and it never knows anything; it is better off than he.'" Ecclesiastes 6:3-5.*

Exodus Has One Passage Dealing with an Accidental Abortion and the Penalty is Civil Payment.

"And if men struggle and strike a woman with child so that she has a miscarriage, yet there is no further injury, he shall be fined as the woman's husband may demand of him, and he shall pay as the judges decide. But if there is any further injury, then you shall appoint as a penalty life for life, eye for eye, tooth for tooth, hand for hand, foot for foot, burn for burn, wound for wound, bruise for bruise." Exodus 21:22-25

Note that if the woman is killed it is a "life for a life," but if the fetus is killed, there is no crime. Get it? Read it carefully for the pro-life anti-abortionists contend further injury is to the fetus, but the distinction in clear. No penalty except civil court payment for the fetus, but the "further injury" refers to the woman. Check it one more time. Babies do not have teeth, so how can there be a tooth for a tooth? Clearly "murder" only applies to the woman and not the fetus.

Chapter 10

Melding Minds and Activities

Finances

Money and its uses are important for preparing for the future. Foolish spending before marriage is a waste to be avoided. By this stage finances should be the subject of discussion if not outright agreement. It is never too early to at least start a joint saving account to prepare for the things needed in the first year of marriage such as home, household goods, cars, life insurance, and medical insurance. If a baby is on the horizon or envisaged, saving is even more important.

Church

Not all churches are equal and not all churches have programs right for young adults. If one partner goes to church in one area and the other goes to a church in another (let's day within a 50 mile radius) it is time to find a church home that both matches the needs of the other and that is more or less halfway between homes. Of course one partner can go to the other's and back and forth, but it is time to limit the distance and compromise on the differences.

Work and Time Management

Work is one of the reasons to get married. Let's say that the man is working nights and the woman is working days. Their time together is limited by work schedules. Distance can add to the lack of time together. Marriage solves the problem by having both return to a safe haven to enjoy the bits of time available as a young couple. If distance is involved, each partner needs to consider a transfer or finding work in the other person's area or half way in between.

Empathy

Understanding the other person's point of view on any of one's own activities while apart is critical. If you fail to communicate what you are doing and if you insist on doing something without the other to see if the other person really trusts you will break a relationship. Always think of the other person when planning an activity such as travel or even seeing a particular movie or going out for a night with same sex friends.

Situation Avoidance

One of the difficult things for single people to realize is that anything that appears to the other to be a situation that involves anyone of the opposite sex is suspect at least and casts doubt on your judgment as a minimum let alone what fuels the imagination. This is true of pictures in which the only ones left at a party are persons of the opposite sex and you. Go back up to empathy. How do you think this is perceived by your "significant other?" Would you want to see him or her surrounded by a person of the opposite sex in a photo? Do you not think that becomes a mental problem for the other?

OK, Does Not Necessarily Mean Approval

The desire to do something "interesting", dangerous, or exciting often drives desire to gain approval from a partner. The partner is then placed in a no win situation. If the partner says no please don't do it, he or she risks loosening the feeling of trust both for the one and the other. If the partner says go ahead, I trust you, the person who mentions the activity feels trusted, but then if the person goes ahead and does it, the other partner feels betrayed even though "official approval" was given.

People in love find things to do together and avoid activities that affect the sensitivities of the other partner.

Staying True

At the stage of melding minds and activities, staying true to each other builds trust. Straying even by going out to a club and dancing with another person, or placing oneself in situations to be noticed by the other sex can end the relationship. Is one night out worth it? Each partner must ask themselves that because they are actually working against themselves. Some people need more social approval than others and go out of their way to encourage looks, comments, and flirting. This is one of those areas where mature judgment is critical and thinking of the emotions of the partner is critical.

Time Outs

This is called giving the other some space. There is nothing wrong with time outs in a relationship as long as they do not last. Young men and women have interests to explore on their own or in the company of same sex friends. The problem is a time out can become permanent. There are no givens.

There is nothing wrong with cooling it for a few weeks or even a couple of months. Absence can make the heart grow fonder, but lengthy time outs mean each partner is vulnerable to approaches by others and loneliness or desire take over the mind and drive one into the arms of a stranger.

I recommend keeping the lines of communication and consulting with each other at least on a weekly basis to determine changes in maturity or shifts in feelings. This is not a check to see who the other is dating, but a status report on progress toward a newly invigorated relationship.

Holidays

At this stage of relationship building integrating the boyfriend and girlfriend in family activities show confidence in each other, pride in showing the other off, and show the family how you feel about each other. Each partner must approach their own set of parents and may have to insist on bringing the other at the risk of the family not having their own son or daughter for the holiday. This soft blackmail effort almost always works.

Goal Setting

1. Engagement Ring

Engagement Rings have a wide range of styles from multiple diamonds to solitaires. Generally they are in gold, white gold, or platinum settings. Diamonds are valued based on color, cut, carat, and clarity, the four C's. Unless someone is rich or careless with resources, a half carat ring or smaller is perfect with a cost under $1,000 without the state and luxury tax. The vast majority of engagement rings sold fall into this category. Cost is one factor, but another one to consider is the practicality of a larger carat (larger stone) ring that can easily get knocked around and be lost.

Commitment is more important than the carat. Having experience and having talked to a lot of couples, I have been told that the attachment even 30 years later is to the original engagement ring regardless of size. Three people told me they would never buy a more expensive replacement even though they had become wealthy. The emotional attachment is too great.

2. Home

The decision on where to live and how much home can a couple afford will take a lot of soul searching. If there are several months between the engagement and the marriage, there is time to save money for a down payment. In today's real estate market a mortgage will probably be under 5%.

Two decades ago when my first daughter was married I insisted they purchase an apartment first. They held it for two or three years and made enough for a down payment on a house in which they still live and it is two-thirds paid for. In 2011 I would now recommend purchasing a home, since real estate prices are so low and a great new three bedroom home can be purchased for under $150,000 even in Southern California.

Renting means paying someone else and not investing wisely if it can be done at all. If both have jobs (to insure against one not having a job or losing one under current economic conditions), or if one makes sufficient income on their own buy a house. Buying also means the mortgage can be written off in taxes. The tax break on a mortgage is still the best deal in America.

There is an old principle: Two can live as cheaply as one. That is true if both would be on their own anyway and would have to pay rent. Why not build for the future.

Even in Southern California a young couple can purchase a house now for a low down payment and low monthly payments under $850 a month. Both parties would spend that amount in rent and then not get the tax break.

There is more. If the house increases in value over time, the husband and wife can sell the house for up to $500,000 in profit (that is above what was paid) and not pay taxes. What a powerful motivator to purchase and not to rent.

3. Savings

How much savings should a young couple have to get engaged? The answer is none, because both will spend it on toys, clothes, trips, and fun things to do. Engagements help because now there is a target date and the couple can use all their resources to put into savings and move in or stay for the time being with relatives increasing the savings account.

One rule of thumb I always recommend is to have enough savings to clear off debt on cars, trucks, boats, and credit cards prior to marriage and then have one year of savings to be able to pay a mortgage and insurance. If one or the other has medical insurance, placing the other person under the plan does not cost that much.

4. Assets

Inventory the assets as to sales value and payments remaining.

Car

Truck

Boat and Trailer

Furniture

Having visualized assets, here is a list to help you prepare an idea of what you really have already. The result is both an inventory and net worth going into the marriage.

List of Assets

Asset	Sales Value	Debt	Comments
Property			Any Owned
Vehicle 1			Car or Truck
Vehicle 2			Car or Truck
Recreational Vehicle(s)			Boat, RV, ATV
Couch			
Easy Chair			
Chairs			
Dining Table and Chairs			
Coffee Table and End Tables			
Appliances			Refrigerator/ Washer/Dryer
Bed			
Dresser			
Desk			
Office Chairs			
Television			
Hot Tub			
Tools			
Computer and Printer			
Patio Furniture			
Engagement Ring/ Wedding Rings			
Jewelry			
China			
Silverware			
Collectibles			
Cash in Bank Accounts			
Savings/CDs/Stock/ Bonds			

This list is not only useful as an inventory and assessment of value (sales value minus debt), but it also is a useful list for determining what is needed after the wedding. China and silverware are often fully taken care of by the wedding gifts as are smaller appliances such as blenders and toasters. On the next page I have a separate table for the purpose of what needs to be bought. Cash and savings are of course deleted on the second form.

The list of things to buy is probably not that great. Consider the assets you already have, the wedding gifts you expect to receive, and ways to purchase carefully. Discuss needs and wants (they are different you know) and then prioritize purchases. You do not want to start in a big hole and then pay the credit card companies. Keep credit at a minimum except for things of value like a house that appreciates over time and provides a roof over the head of the family.

List of Things to Buy

Asset	Cost	Credit?	Comments
Property			Any Owned
Vehicle 1			Car or Truck
Vehicle 2			Car or Truck
Recreational Vehicle(s)			Boat, RV, ATV
Couch			
Easy Chair			
Chairs			
Dining Table and Chairs			
Coffee Table and End Tables			
Appliances			Refrigerator/ Washer/Dryer
Bed			
Dresser			
Desk			
Office Chairs			
Television			
Tools			
Computer and Printer			
Patio Furniture			
China			
Silverware			
Cookware			
Bathroom Items			
Work Clothes			

By going through this exercise couples will see they have a lot more assets than they realized, but they will also understand the money needed to purchase the rest of the items necessary for setting up a household.

5. Budget

A budget is very simple to set up, but agreement may be harder. The budget looks at income, savings, and payments. When I got married, I allocated by thirds: one third for car and car maintenance, one third for rent/mortgage and one third for food, clothes, eating out, and recre4ation. That principle still looks pretty good. For one thing, the maximum mortgage ranges around 30% or almost a third of a monthly budget. Cars and vehicles and their maintenance are usually about a third, leaving the other third for the rest. If they are paid off going into the marriage that allows another third of income to be used either in savings or in setting up the household assuming there were no savings to do so. Here is a list of typical monthly costs.

Monthly Expenses and Income			
Monthly Bills	**Account #**	**Address**	**Month**
Mortgage Include Insurance			750
Home Equity Loan			100
Auto Loan			350
Vehicle Loan			250
Water/Sewer/Trash			50
Student Loan			100
Electric			100
Gas			30
Cable/Internet/Phone			120
Food/Clothes			400
Insurance Cars/Vehicles			100
Medical Insurance			200
Home Maintenance			50
Credit Card Payments			100
Total Cash Outflow			2,700
Income After Taxes			3,500
Cash Remaining for Savings			800
Added if loans paid (See below)			700
Discretionary Income			1,500

Assume going into the marriage that during the engagement period, the loans have been paid off along with credit cards and that there are no remaining student loans. The added savings or discretionary income is now $1,500 a month on a total income by both parties of $3,500 after taxes. With the mortgage and home equity lines tax deductible, the couple will also get back a couple of thousand from the IRS giving them a total discretionary income for the year of $20,000. In other words the couple could make it on $28,000 a year, because the total cash outflow on the chart drops to $2,000 per month meaning bills for the year including food and everything is $24,000.

Chapter 11

Adjustment and Engagement: Final Boarding

Final Preparations for Engagement

You have reached the final boarding stages for you flight into the future. Deciding one has consciously or subconsciously obtained sufficient information about a future marriage partner is personal. Some feel they have it on the first date, but is it wise to jump in a new airplane without testing it first? "God may be your copilot," but it is better if He is the pilot and you're the copilot.

Don't Compromise, Adjust

A compromise can make both relational partners believe they have given up too much. There is a better way. While there must be give and take in a relationship, a better way to work together is to adjust. I am going to make a strong case that an adjustment is not a compromise, but a better way to cope.

An adjustment is moving closer in a relationship without surrendering principles, morals, or beliefs. There are some areas that couples cannot adjust and compromise may make one or the other feel defeated. Put those in a box and close the lid, but make sure they are not the kinds of things that will cause marital problems after the wedding. Whether or not have premarital sex is a specific area that comes to mind that can cause one or the other relational partner anxiety. That is precisely the kind of thing that if one relational partner has a strong belief or principle against premarital sex, can easily be put in a little box, because the issue is gone with the first wedding night in any case.

Some Relatively Easy Adjustments

Work Location

Transfer and relocate to new work area closest to the partner. This is not a compromise. This is a rational adjustment to place each in closer proximity, which at the very least saves gas and mileage for both. Some work locations cannot be helped and some require long distance travel. I can start with military assignments and move to traveling salesmen.

If proximity cannot be attained prior to marriage, this is an area that can be settled over time through the engagement and marriage. Military wives gain an entire support team when they get married to someone in the military and traveling salesmen can adjust their territories with successful performance and limit their absence.

Church Home

Agree on a denomination: This is a major area for Christians if one is a Baptist or Protestant (there is a difference between the two) and one is a Roman Catholic. The Roman Catholic is still bound to have a marriage in the Roman Catholic church and promises to raise the subsequent children in the Roman Catholic faith. These two principles tend to lose a lot of potential families to the Catholic Church.

Agree on a church/synogogue location: A location halfway between the two partners in terms of distance is ideal while in a premarital relationship. This is another one of those little box issues that is settled after marriage, since both will want to go to the same church together.

Alternating churches or synagogues: The third adjustment that can be made is to alternate church attendance together, but it is important that both go to each other's church if this is the adjustment.

Maximize Together Time

Adjust schedules: Adjusting schedules should be something both relational partners want to do. Past habits and past schedules can be adjusted to find more time together and keep the bond close.

Adjust friends: In a relationship an adjustment of friends may have to be made. Single friends no longer relate well and may actively or passively interfere out of jealousy for the relationship and selfishness for losing time with their "best friend." Couples doing things together is the right way to go such as to a beach or resort, boat riding, going to church together, or partying together.

Adjust "Hang Out" time: I am from another generation, but hate the term, "I am going to hang out" either with a relational partner or with friends. "Hang up" is more appropriate, since something is holding up the relationship if one is always "hanging out" with friends. A relationship requires attention and "hanging out" takes away from that relationship. This is an area that is difficult to approach the other partner and ask them to give up their present affiliations and going to the homes of friends, but as a mature adult, the "hang out time can be used both for more attention for the partner and for productive enterprises in preparation for marriage.

Set dates: Even for the seasoned relational couple, each should set surprise dates and exciting adventures to keep the relationship fresh. Inviting the partner to the parents home is great for presenting a united front and aiding the integrative process into family affairs. Going to see Christmas lights in December is a wonderful happy tour that can be made. The list is endless, but you have the idea.

Engagement

The time finally comes for getting engaged. You may be in a committed relationship, but the next step is engagement, a far more personal and final preparatory phase for marriage. Am I ready for the next step you ask yourself? So far you have used the pages of this Christian Guide to your advantage. You found the perfect match after recognizing the magnets. You have made a complete assessment of each other and resources to be shared.

Dating experts do not agree on when together is together, let alone when to get engaged. The purpose of dating has been fulfilled. That is not just to make an assessment, but to provide time to work out where to work, where to live, when to have children, saving money for the things needed to start a household, and planning for the engagement time and setting a date for the wedding.

Now it is time to move the relationship to the final takeoff and landing. In western cultures the material representation is the engagement ring for the finger of the girl/woman which says you have committed to one and one only for the future. Engagement ring selection, purchase, and presentation are all highly personal. The longer the premarital relationship, the more consultation may be needed. Surprises are great, but rejections are devastating.

Engagement Readiness

There are clues from each relational partner that need to be read. I venture to state unequivocally that the female partner is ready anytime after two years. You will find that I used this cutoff date for several aspects of a premarital relationship. That is my arbitrary choice for illustrative purposes. What are some clues? I will list some of the more obvious:

Engagement Discussion: Discussions about becoming engaged are an obvious clue. Both parties can carefully sense out the partners ideas about a more permanent relationship and attain a reasonable certainty that engagement will be welcomed at some soon to be determined time, hopefully after the lists and inventories in the previous chapter.

Jewelry Store Shopping: While walking in a mall, the girlfriend "accidentally" walks by or into a Jewelry store and begins looking at engagement rings. Do you need a stronger clue, men? Well I have on for you next.

Taste in Rings: While in a jewelry store, the girlfriend says, I love that particular ring the most. Certainty has dawned even on the most dense men.

Ring Finger Size: Men, do not purchase the wrong size ring. If you have not been given the specifications, see if you can just take the box for the presentation and return the ring for another size. There is really no substitute, however, for knowing the ring size.

Wedding Thoughts: The girlfriend hints that weddings in June are nice and that is the month that she would like to get married. Now you have a time frame with which to work.

Engagement Ring Purchase

One way to insure the ring size is correct, the choice or ring is correct, and the engagement is certain is to purchase the ring with your girlfriend in tow. If you think this is not romantic, how about first taking your girlfriend on a smash up date to a wonderful restaurant with a view or one that has significant memories for the both of you. Then tell her you have a surprise waiting for her.

Make a reservation date at the jewelers prior to the wonderful evening with the jeweler ready to assist you with the ring placed in 24-hour reserve that you believe to be the right one and take your girlfriend there for fitting. If for some reason it does not fit properly, or if she changed her mind as to style, the adjustment can be made on the spot. She will be thrilled with your practicality and thoughtfulness at the same time.

Engagement Ring Presentation

Assuming that the engagement ring presentation is not at the jewelers, anything goes. Just don't hide it in candy or cake, since it could be lost or swallowed. The American custom is to get down onw one knee, hold the hand of the intended, and ask the question, "Will you marry me." There is no reason you cannot do it at the jewelers while trying on the ring.

Subsequent Proposals if Needed

Remember our study of persistence? A first turndown does not mean it is over. Acceptance of another date is in itself an indicator of continuing interest and future success. The first turndown may have been because the woman simply was not yet ready to let go of independence and commit, or she wishes to observe more maturity or correction of some problem she perceives in the relationship.

Change locations for certain. Bring flowers or take her to full course date including meal, movie or show, and a romantic walk on the beach. By now the man should be able to judge when the woman is the most ready and softest in her ways. A sober proposal and acceptance is necessary. Clear heads are needed.

Engagement Announcement

Announcing the engagement can be a major production or an informal one. Formal engagement announcements can be prepared and sent out to friends and family announcing the happy event, but usually announcements are more informal with the formal announcements saved for the wedding invitations. Informal announcement should be as inclusive as possible:

Relatives: Moms, dads, brothers, and sisters are usually the first to be told. They take great pleasure in further spreading of the word. Excitement reigns in the household and suddenly the prospect of planning a wedding generates amazing enthusiasm. The best of all worlds is for both the son or daughter and their fiancée to be together to receive the congratulations and show the wedding ring. This makes parents feel comfortable of the strength of the relationship.

Friends: Friends are usually the next ones to find out as phone calls tell the happy story.

Work Associates: The next day after the engagement, work associates will see the diamond ring on the hand of the female fiancée and starting celebrating, or in some cases slinking off into a corner. The male fiancée begins to tell his boss and coworkers of the engagement as a means of defending both himself and his fiancée.

Social Networks: If the "in a relationship" block has not been checked, go straight to the Engaged block. Even better is a picture of the happy couple and the wedding ring held up for inspection.

Rules of Engagement

If you have not done so during the "relationship stage" now is the time to close down relations with others and eliminate outside interference from supposed "friends." Remember earlier how my wife found my box of pictures of previous girlfriends and burned the box? She was right. Burn old relationships even if we think they are just nice to remember items. The focus is now on each other—just two in a circle. Too often we are naïve and think nothing ourselves of the strings to the past, but at least consider the feelings of the other.

Sharing and Caring:

Sharing: The newly engaged couple has a need for sharing their happiness as far and wide as possible and need to appear together in media and in person. In small towns and even some larger ones, an engagement is announced in the local paper along with a picture of the happy couple. Newspapers are always interested in providing this service free of charge with a write up accompanying the photo.

Newly engaged couples should also be together when showing off their ring for the first time to parents and relatives while receiving the accolades for the wonderful news. Prospective mothers-in-law often get to hug the fiancée for the first time and welcome them personally into the family.

Spreading the news through networks of friends, coworkers, and others that may or may not have an interest is desirable. Motives are pure because now the couple is a special unit. Social networks, the new phenomenon of the Internet are a great way to let those who had a past interest of any kind in on the news.

Caring: Caring though now must be focused on cutting off the past after a short space of time, such as a week or two. Everything is changed. Attitudes understandably are changed and the couple now must build their protective barriers together. This is not a time for accusation, but observation of each other's external relationships and discussion of how to relate to the past people outside closest friends and relatives.

Caring Tasks to Perform

Task #1: Separation from Past Friends:
There are different categories of friends.

Category A: True Friends. One way to determine true friends is to see if they congratulate you for the engagement. Those are most likely a higher category of friend and are worth consideration for keeping as long as they are recognized as not falsely praising the engagement.

Category B: Ignorers. If they ignore the announcement, they are good candidates for elimination from friendship consideration and from network exchanges.

Category C: Negative Responders or Jokers. Of course any negative responders or those who jeer and jest about the engagement must be gone immediately.

Category D: Associates. These are not necessarily friends, but just people with whom one associates because of the work place, student affiliation, church affiliation, or business and marketing association.

Category E: Game players. Game players are entrapment specialists. Avoid them.

Category F: Opposite Sex "Friends." Get rid of them. Do not accept new ones just because they are "friends" with your fiancée.

Task #2: Prune the Social Network Tree:
Prune the social network now if not done previously! Get rid of potential sour grapes and those who would try to interfere. Get rid of past flames or flings. Think about each person remaining in your network and how your fiancée may look at them or how writing any comments to them might injure their feelings.

Pruning the tree is important not just for the sake of each other, but for the perceptions of those who may be privileged to view the network and for those who may be assessing the strength of the engagement. Do not write "I like/love what you said," or anything at all to a person of the opposite sex on your network. Get rid of them in the first place. Prune the tree!

Task #3: Stop Attending "Most" Parties Unless the Fiancée is Invited

Social habits are one of the things that must be broken after engagement. Notice I used the word "most" because judgment is involved.

Category A: All Same Sex Parties. If there is an all male or all female birthday party, then the word "most" comes into play because there will be no one of the opposite sex there anyway, so that is higher on the permissive list, although personally my recommendation is not to attend any party without the fiancée. That one is a choice and judgment is involved.

Category B: Office/Business/Association Parties. Office, business, or association (Student/Political/Class) parties are a difficult category for judgment as well. The person invited to an office or business party should at least request that their fiancée be allowed to come to the party. If that is rejected and there is a real need to put in face time, have the fiancée drive you to the party, have them go to the mall or movie, and pick you up at a specified time. This strengthens perceptions in the office of the seriousness of the engagement and assures you are not the last one at the party by the design of others.

Other than those two categories stop attending parties without the fiancée!

Engagement Planning Toward Marriage

Now is the time for a final inventory and then prepare for marriage. The checklist at the end of the book provides a comprehensive inventory and planning guide. The engaged couple also needs to ask themselves, "Let's see, what do we have in common, what do we need to work on, how can I improve myself, how can I communicate I am ready for a wedding?" Christians have three power sources. church, prayer, and Bible study. That puts Christians ahead of the game already.

Attending church together sets the tone for courtship, relationships in a healthy manner, and a shared experience. Prayer not only changes things, it protects relationships by setting oneself right and then praying for the other partner. Bible study one night per week continues to bring people not only closer to God, but closer to each other. You have a predetermined destination, now enjoy the ride.

Natural Conflict with Parents

Girlfriends are in natural conflict with the boyfriend's mother and boys in conflict with the girlfriend's father. The reason for conflict of girlfriends with boyfriend's mothers is that in some way the mother feels displaced in the relationship and the girlfriend feels she is competing for the affections of the boyfriend with a same sex person. The conflict is normally health as a way to detach the boyfriend from others and over time both the girlfriend and mother accommodate to each other.

I thought for years that my wife was in conflict with my mother, until one day my wife said how much she loved my mother, valued her opinion, and was uplifted by her spiritual wisdom. I was in shock! I never thought the two would see eye to eye on anything.

Boyfriends have a different task when relating to the father of the girlfriend. The boy is now in physical and mental competition in the eyes of the father with him and the father is naturally concerned about how the boy will treat his daughter and can the boy provide for the daughter.

What is Love?

"What is Love?" is another reference to a song title. The question, however, is a powerful one. It demands an appropriate answer. Let me give you one based on what the Bible says. The Bible has the best definition for love ever written. Poets and musicians have tried to improve it through the centuries. Plays, movies, television series, have been devoted to defining it. Yet I have never seen the equal to God's word. I have taken the liberty to write a Love Poem based on the words of I Corinthians, Chapter 13, one of the greatest passages in the Bible after John 3:16. I cannot improve it. I can only adapt it for contemporary understanding.

THE LOVE POEM

Based on I Corinthians Chapter 13

Roy E. Peterson,

From Between Darkness and Light. AuthorHouse. March 2011

> Love's forever patient, love's forever kind.
> Love does not envy, no boast will you find.
> Love is not proud and love is not rude.
> Love's not self-seeking, or has anger that's crude.
>
> Wrongs aren't recorded, nor in evil delight.
> Love seeks the truth and rejoices in right.
> Love will protect and always will trust.
> Love always hopes, perseveres, and adjusts.
>
> Prophecies will cease and tongues will be stilled.
> Knowledge will perish and fates will be sealed.
> We see rather poorly in the darkened mirror
> The heavenly truths we know to be purer.
>
> When time has ended and we meet face to face,
> How humble we'll be as He gives us His grace.
> Faith, hope, and love are the three that remain,
> But the greatest is love as we're born again.

Chapter 12

On Board and Ready for Takeoff

Wedding Visions

Planning

More good news, men. Unless you are running away to get married, the bride's family pays for the wedding gown and the cost of the wedding—generally. This depends on sufficient family income to afford to pay $10,000 to $15,000 for a wedding. I have known negotiations to take place that with a simple wedding such as a small church wedding, pool side, Oceanside, or rose garden, $10,000 for the larger wedding would be given as a gift to the bride and groom.

Allow six months after engagement minimum to plan a wedding. Again the bride and her mother normally take over. That does not mean the guys sit on the sidelines. The bride and her mother will want to consult on everything from the location and size of the wedding to the choice of flowers.

The groom's side gets to pay for the rehearsal dinner and the honeymoon.

Wedding Invitation

A sample wedding invitation is not as easy to construct as in the past. That is because divorced parents are often involved and the wording starts to get complicated. Here is a sample with divorced parents:

Mr. and Mrs. Xxxxxxx
and
Mr. and Mrs. Xxxxxxx
Request the honor of your presence
At the marriage of the daughter of Mrs. Xxxxx and
Mr. Xxxxxxxx
First Name Second Name
to
First Name, Second Name, Last Name
as they join their hands in holy matrimony
Saturday, June 7, 2011
7 o'clock in the Evening
At XXX Church
Address
City, State

Reception to follow in the fellowship hall

From Here to Eternity

Proverbs 18:22 tells us:

The man who finds a wife finds a treasure, and he receives favor from the LORD. (NLT)

Many of us remember the Movie, <u>From Here to Eternity</u>. Everyone wants happiness and everyone wants a fairy tale to turn out right. So it is with weddings. That is the final setting for vows that should last a lifetime. If the man and wife have chosen wisely, listened to their hearts, and picked the right mate, the world can go away and love remains regardless of circumstances.

How do we get "from here to eternity?" Christian living and obeying God's commands are the strongest way to get there. It starts with the wedding vows. <u>About.com</u> has four traditional wedding vows and they reflect the strength of the pledged word:

Traditional Wedding Vows

Examples of Wedding Vows That Are Timeless Classics

By Nina Callaway, <u>About.com Guide</u>

Traditional Wedding Vows 1:

I, (name), take you (name), to be my (wife/husband), to have and to hold from this day forward, for better or for worse, for richer, for poorer, in sickness and in health, to love and to cherish; from this day forward until death do us part.

Traditional Wedding Vows 2:

I, (name), take you, (name), to be my [opt: lawfully wedded] (husband/wife), my constant friend, my faithful partner and my love from this day forward. In the presence of God, our family and friends, I offer you my solemn vow to be your faithful partner in sickness and in health, in good times and in bad, and in joy as well as in sorrow. I promise to love you unconditionally, to support you in your goals, to honor and respect you, to laugh with you and cry with you, and to cherish you for as long as we both shall live.

Traditional Wedding Vows 3 (traditional civil ceremony vows):

(Name), I take you to be my lawfully wedded (husband/wife). Before these witnesses I vow to love you and care for you as long as we both shall live. I take you with all your faults and your strengths as I offer myself to you with my faults and strengths. I will help you when you need help, and I will turn to you when I need help. I choose you as the person with whom I will spend my life.

Traditional Wedding Vows 4:

I, (name), take you, (name), to be my beloved (wife/husband), to have and to hold you, to honor you, to treasure you, to be at your side in sorrow and in joy, in the good times, and in the bad, and to love and cherish you always. I promise you this from my heart, for all the days of my life.

Have and to Hold: To have and to hold is exclusivity. You belong to each other. You were meant for each other. You are the perfect fit and therefore perfect pair. No one else can have you. No one else can hold you. Having means living together and sharing. Holding means caressing, fondling, and intercourse.

Better or Worse: Better or worse means that there will be tests and trials in a marriage. We like the better part because that speaks of starting a family, doing fun things together, and just being with each other. The worse part is the problem. Worse means facing obstacles together and overcoming them. It means discussions, idea sharing, and problem solving. But no matter how good it is or how bad it is you are together in this and that makes all the difference.

Richer, Poorer: There should be something in here about sufficiency, but the two extremes of being richer or being poorer are presented. Each condition has its own set of problems. Being rich does not assure happiness, just as being poor does not mean there cannot be a rich life in other ways.

Sickness and Health: Women are much better equipped to handle the sick part. That is because of the nurturing nature of women and their family protection skills ingrained in them from childhood. Studies have shown mother's surprisingly are more attuned to the sickness of a daughter than of a son. Maybe that has something to do with it.

Love and Cherish: Love is obvious, but what is cherish? Cherish means to show great tenderness for someone or thing, to treasure someone or thing, and to cling fondly to someone or thing. Let's get rid of the "thing." I like the word "cling." Clinging means holding on for dear life under any circumstances. Sailors cling to pieces of wood from a sunken ship. Entrepreneurs cling to hope for their business to grow. Women and men cling together and only to each other when the storms of life assail them. I like the "love unconditionally" in the second traditional vow. That says a lot and is powerful.

Forsaking All Others: This one has clarity. In the Christian centered life, the principle of abundant living is forsaking all others and holding on to each other or the "clinging" principles just discussed. Exclusion is the first thought that come to mind. Others are excluded from the circle of two. In case you are thinking about previous boyfriends and girlfriends, you are properly oriented. But it also means leaving the family nest, flying like a pair of birds together and building your own nest.

Chapter 13

The Right Stuff

OK! So I WATCHED one too many Tom Cruise Movies. We have covered preflight boarding, preparation for takeoff, and are now flying. This is where the "right stuff" comes into play.

Night One: Start of Honeymoon

Unless parents have given tickets to a resort somewhere in the world, the choice of a honeymoon location is up to the newly married couple. Of course the decision of where to go has been a month or two in advance. Deciding on the location and length of the honeymoon is a function of family resources and real world costs after the honeymoon. Men, a real one to two week honeymoon is essential.

I remember that I had planned a one night honeymoon between where I got married and my place of work. I intended to keep working to take care of real expenses. My bride had other thoughts. After the first night, she started asking, "Where are we going on our honeymoon?" We had never discussed it and I was convinced just being with me was enough. It wasn't. I responded to her question, "We are." She replied, "No we are not and I am going somewhere for a week myself if you do not adjust now." Uhhh, OK. I called my place of work and told them I needed to take a honeymoon. The boss said they already planned for that even though I had not asked. I made immediate arrangements for a destination 300 miles away that honeymooners often visited, but was not expensive. We made it. The honeymoon was a great time of sharing not just physically, but connecting emotionally. I found out a lot about my bride I did not know.

The lesson is that a honeymoon is essential in establishing a future emotional connection and thinking together about the future in terms you cannot understand without the honeymoon. The two of you need some time away from everyone and everything and get to enjoy a special time in your life.

In planning a honeymoon, of course the first consideration is resources. After that is adjusting and agreeing jointly on the ideal spot. I suggest a simple exercise of each party listing the following ideas for a honeymoon.

1. Location Type: Beach, Mountains, Resort, Dude Ranch. Note I suggest not listing a specific place of which you are thinking, but surveying your partner's ideal location type. Then you can be the first to spring the brilliant spur of the moment idea of them with , "How about xxx?"

2. Cost: Available resources as seen by each partner

3. Time: Availability from work or school

4. Entertainment: Things to do and share doing with pleasure

5. Travel: Plane, car, train, cruise ship

6. Accommodations: Hotel, motel, rented facility

7. Romantic Appeal: Warm, inviting, secluded, views

Now let me take you through an exercise with Romeo and Juliet, our old friends. First let's consider the things they came up with in common and then look at where the adjustments have to be made and common agreement reached.

Honeymoon Exercise

Idea	Juliet	Romeo
Location	Resort on warm beach	Resort on warm beach
Cost	$4,000	$2,000
Time	2 weeks	1 week (cost consideration)
Entertainment	Swimming, boating, sea shells	Scuba diving
Travel	Air	Air
Accommodations	Honeymoon special hotel	Quiet and low key
Romantic Appeal	Palm trees, tropical breezes, View to the western setting sun	Wicker furniture, trees, sandy beach

Romeo and Juliet could literally take this list to a travel advisor who could serve as a kind of arbiter and make recommendations both would love at the same time. The fit is not that exceptional and in the real world often is very close to what both want anyway, since they have been doing things with each other. Given resource considerations, the travel agent would probably advise something in North or Central America. The agent might offer three options: Acapulco, Belize, or Cabo San Lucas for two weeks at $3,000 for the pair including air fare.

Sex as a married couple is new even if both have had premarital sex or prior experience. Remember it takes up to 20 minutes to be sure the female is sufficiently stimulated for mind blowing intercourse. After the first orgasm, they come in much shorter periods with some women experiencing multiple orgasms. That is the goal for the man.

When done right, the honeymoon is a memory that will last a lifetime. It is a place you may want to revisit on occasion to renew those first feelings of married connectedness and romance.

A Few Days Later

I almost forgot. We had to give Romeo and Juliet a honeymoon and day two is not the time to start on an agenda, except the outlines of an agenda can begin to form during the honeymoon. There has to be something besides pleasure to discuss. Right?

From day one in a marriage there are some agenda items on which the couple needs to come to an agreement. I used to puzzle over the words in the Bible that pastors said a man had to dominate. Few modern marriages resemble the domination principle, except for the physical protection afforded by the husband to the wife. Men need to get it through their heads that they are not going to dominant all facets of a marriage. Women do have equal standing.

Equality and Sharing in a Marriage: What gets shared? I will give you a starter list: money, housework, maintenance, vehicles, time, work, problems, difficulties, child rearing, assets, food, each other.

Decision-Making in a Marriage: Decisions are made together. If the husband always gets his way, the equality principle goes out the window. Decisions are a shared responsibility and the ideas of each spouse are laid on the table for inspection. The amount of decision-making entrusted to the man is a function of how much a woman is willing to trust his instincts and plan.

Goal Setting in a Marriage: Time for another list. What goals need to be set? Actually it is better to list the goals before the marriage during the engagement period, but if they have not yet been done or completed, now is the time. Goals should be realistic and reachable. Goals need to be tangible. That is they need to have a number or event associated with them. They need to be fair and impartial. Goals need an expected time of achievement. Goals should be visual. Goals need to be set for short term, medium, and long range. Here is my suggested list:

1. Number of children
2. Career(s)
3. Savings
4. Investments
5. Vacation destinations
6. Lifestyle
7. Vehicles needed
8. Area in which to live
9. Future home or Stay
10. Church to Attend

In one of my real estate courses, I was taught to select pictures representing my goals and put them on one page for review and updating.

Since that time I have reviewed my goals every December for carry over into the next year and have cut out pictures to represent my goals. I have been amazed by what I can accomplish once I have a focus.

Goals are important. Expressing them and writing them makes them concrete. Accomplishing them strengthens the marriage. I left the ten suggested goal discussion s blank after presenting the short title. That is because what they are and how you work them out is up to you, the couple. No one else should advise on the goals, only the methods to get there, such as an investment broker.

A Hope and a Prayer

My greatest hope is that young couples fully comprehend the weight of decisions made to go on a date, construct a serious relationship centered on each other and their faith, and choose the right path for their relationship with the appropriate goals in mind of engagement and marriage. I hope the couple reserves themselves physically for each other, which amplifies the pleasure of sexual intercourse when it is decided it is the right time, keeps out the ones that are seeking to destroy the pure and the good, and makes the wedding night extra special.

My fervent prayer is that the objective information and presentation in <u>Magnetism to Marriage</u> is a practical guide for young couples and is the only guide needed from dating to the wedding night. The short discussion of how to achieve maximum pleasure in sexual intercourse for a woman is not a replacement for a sex manual, but it surely is presented more with empathy and care than a sex manual can do. I pray couples use the information wisely and look to divine guidance.

This Day Forward: **Here we go! Takeoff! "From here to eternity!"**

Paradise Island the Next Stop.

One more detail – A check list for all plans and decisions.

Chapter 14

Checklist for Planning and Decision Making

PLANS ARE FUN THINGS to do for a couple in a relationship and incorporate all the past, present, and future hopes and dreams of each man and woman, but decisions are a serious commitment to each other and require some adjustments. Practical limitations in terms of money and capabilities are moderators of the hopes and dreams, but need not limit the long term goals of the couple. By that I mean the couple must be practical about how they will begin married life, but long term goals can be set at five to ten years out about what the couple wants to accomplish.

Two can actually live more cheaply than one for a number of reasons.

1. Single people eat out a lot and waste two-thirds of their money doing so, when in a marriage they eat together and save tremendously, even with eating out once or twice a week.

2. Married couples do more things in the home together. For example, rather than going out to a movie they are more satisfied to rent a movie, watch television or work together on what they both like to do.

3. Gas is saved because the couple now has one location rather than driving distances to see each other.

4. Purchasing a home saves money over renting. Monthly cost is likely the same or less. Real savings is on income tax with a deduction for interest that almost cuts the monthly payment in half over renting.

5. The income tax rate is less for a married couple than for each single person and there are more combined deductions.

6. Marriage moderates each other's expenditures and reduces gifts to others.

This <u>Practical Guide</u> focuses on the perfection of the premarital relationship and start of a marriage and not the longer term direction in which the couple may wish to work. Column one is the hope or dream. Column two incorporates practical considerations needed to adjust the dream to reality. Column three is blank for the decision of the couple. Couples may continue to discuss the ramifications and change the decision up to the point they actually complete the task.

Dreams to Reality Plan and Decision Checklist

Dream	Practical Considerations	Decision
Work Place	1. Move, stay, or adjust to maximize income and maximize time together 2. One or both work (often both start by working, or the man is often supported by the wife until he completes education or training for a position)	
Time Together	1. How to maximize premarital time 2. How to maximize engagement time 3. How to maximize wedded life time	
Church Location	1. Church denomination or type 2. Move, stay, or adjust and when	
Vehicles	1. Type needed for work and family planning 2. Pay off in advance if possible	

Engagement Ring	1. Man: Consult with intended fiancée, or hope the choice is right 2. Woman: Any indications in advance to lead the man in the right direction 3. Style, size, cost, gold or silver/ platinum	
Ring Presentation	1. Any presentation anywhere is romantic 2. Location of presentation: Start with the general and work to the specific 3. Setting the mood (restaurant/ beach/first date) 4. Style of presentation (on knees is used less these days in favor of hiding it in something, such as another gift, or easily discoverable place and then directing the attention of the woman to the place)	
Engagement Announcement	1. Official announcement? 2. Communication to relatives and then friends 3. Social network communication changes and deletion of so called "friends"	
Bank Savings Account	1. Savings goal before marriage 2. Choice of whether or not to combine all money before marriage	
Wedding Type	1. Church, chapel, Pastor, Justice of the Peace 2. Indoor or outdoor, beach, garden 3. Big, small, number of invitees (approximate)	
Wedding Location	1. Usually choice of the bride to be 2. Considerations: distance and availability	

Wedding Dress	1. Bride to be choice without male input 2. Bride's family normally pays	
Wedding Date/ Time	1. Start with approximate month as target. Add time of day, and then select a date. 2. Reserve the date immediately, since the couple may be competing for the appointed date and time.	
Wedding Gifts	1. Registration for china, silver, and crystal? 2. Open gifting?	
Wedding Medical	1. Blood work required for wedding license 2. Woman may wish to have hymen removed to eliminate initial discomfort on wedding night	
Wedding License	Required in each state	
Rehearsal Dinner	Man's family decides and pays	
Wedding Ceremony	1. Who officiates? Make sure to ask and lock up the date 2. Select the vows 3. Number of Maids of Honor and Groomsmen 4. Best man and Bridesmaid choice 5. Who gives away the bride in the ceremony 6. Seating for relatives (usually one set on one side and one on the other).	

Wedding Details	1. Brides colors	
	2. Floral arrangements	
	3. Bouquet selection	
	4. Brides maid dress selection style and colors	
	5. Groom attire: Tux or suit or appropriate type and color	
	6. Music selection	
	7. Who will sing and what?	
	8. Wedding rehearsal and lock in the date by reservation	
	9. Wedding announcement type and number of guests	
Wedding Reception	1. Size depends on size of the hall rented	
	2. Wedding cake size, taste, decorations	
	3. Music: live band, DJ, Party Planners	
	4. Food and Refreshments	
	5. Dance or not	
	6. Bar or not	
	7. Time of departure for honeymoon	

Honeymoon	1. Distance may dictate time of wedding 2. First night stay may need to be close to the wedding location and then departure set the next day 3. Budgeted amount 4. Length of time for honeymoon often dictated by work requirements and time available 5. Select preference for type of resort or area such as beach location or sightseeing location 6. Then select continent 7. Then select amenities desired such as scuba diving, etc. 8. Narrow the choice to three and check the price and right time of year to go there (depends on wedding date) 9. Prepare clothes 10. Plan the days' events	
Home Type	1. Single story or multistory, apartment or house 2. Size 3. Rent or buy 4. Brick, Stucco, Wood 5. Roof type: Tile, Shake, Asphalt 6. Color and trim	

Home Needs	1. Number of Bedrooms and baths
	2. Extra Garage Space for husband to work?
	3. Home Office (may be the extra bedroom)
	4. Yard, Fence, Grass, Pool, Hot Tub, Trees, Garden
	5. Kitchen requirements
Home Location	1. First select the area
	2. Then select the most affordable homes to view based on anticipated budget considering income and expenses
	3. Then select the best school district for the most affordable home
	4. Then check out the neighborhood before purchase such as consult with the police department on crime statistics for neighborhoods and check databases for known sex offenders
	5. Select an experienced realtor from a nationally known brand or well regarded local one
	6. Narrow the choice to three
	7. Review everything on all three
	8. Select
	9. Expect to put down an earnest money deposit of $2,000 to $5,000 on moderate cost homes to be refunded at purchase or added to the down payment
	Note: the speed of decision making depends on the number of days the property is on the market and the economy of the area selected

Furniture	1. Style adjustment comes first 2. Color comes second 3. Amount desired, but start simply 4. Furniture in existence prior to marriage and available to bring to the home	
Furnishings	1. Color combinations 2. Interior and exterior paint 3. Window treatments 4. Appliances 5. Carpeting style and color	
Pets	Type and purpose	
Children	1. Ideal number and sex of children 2. Approximate time to start the family	
Financial Planning	1. Savings 2. Assets 3. Investments 4, Income and Expenses 5. Budget 6. Credit	